Baseline Assessment

Practice, Problems and Possibilities

Geoff Lindsay and Martin Desforges

2004

David Fulton Publishers
London

David Fulton Publishers Ltd
Ormond House, 26–27 Boswell Street, London WC1N 3JD

First published in Great Britain by David Fulton Publishers 1998

Reprinted 1999

Note: The right of Geoff Lindsay and Martin Desforges to be identified as the authors of this work has been asserted by them in accordance with the Copyright, Designs and Patents Act 1988.

Copyright © Geoff Lindsay and Martin Desforges 1998

British Library Cataloguing in Publication Data
A catalogue record for this book is available from the British Library

ISBN 1–85346–514–3

Typeset by Textype Typesetters, Cambridge
Printed in Great Britain by Antony Rowe Ltd., Chippenham, Wiltshire

Contents

Dedication

To our children

Preface

Baseline assessment became compulsory from September 1998. Enshrined in the Education Act 1997, and subject to cross party support, baseline assessment has high popularity – at least in principle. Baseline assessment grew out of earlier schemes to identify children with difficulties in an attempt to prevent or ameliorate the effects of these problems on later educational progress. In addition, such approaches were developed to aid the planning of learning experiences for all children. When determined by teachers and support staff, including advisers and educational psychologists, these schemes were clearly targeted at enhancing children's development.

This was still the general aim of the government's baseline assessment as it was set out in the early documentation, the Education Bill and indeed the Education Act 1997. In practice, however, the focus of interest has altered, greater importance being attributed to school accountability. Baseline assessment is seen as the means to permit 'value-added' measures of children's progress during the Infant stage to be calculated, and so enable schools' contributions to educational development to be assessed.

The Qualifications and Curriculum Authority distributed guidance on baseline assessment in the summer of 1998, including a list of accredited schemes and further information on the QCA's scales. The schemes discussed in Chapter 5 are all accredited, although not all meet the criteria in their earlier format. However, this guidance does not directly affect the arguments we make. There is, for example, still no requirement that baseline assessment schemes must provide evidence of adequate technical quality. There remains a commitment to allow any scheme which meets the criteria (see pages 12–13) to be accredited for use by schools. We welcome the QCA's intention to review evaluation evidence when accreditation is up for review in about 2000/2001, but we are concerned about the indications that the QCA inclines more to a single scheme, so emphasising the focus on value-added and accountability, and relegating the importance of the collaborative work which has resulted in the wealth of schemes available in the first year of the compulsory system. There is a tension between the use of baseline assessment for formative purposes, which we believe to be the interest of most teachers, and for summative purposes, in this case value-added analyses, which we believe to the priority of the government.

In this book we shall review these different elements and purposes, and their implications for practice. We shall review the educational, psychological and psychometric factors which are relevant to developing baseline assessment, and consider the socio-political context in which these initiatives are occurring.

We should declare an interest. As teachers, educational psychologists and researchers we have been committed to practice which is based on evidence rather than good intentions. The assessment of children's progress from school entry is to be welcomed, but it must be carried out carefully and accurately, with a clear understanding of purpose. The present baseline assessment initiative, while having many good features, also has serious flaws. It is our purpose to aid those with an interest in baseline assessment to appreciate its worth and limitations, in order that children's educational development might be optimised.

Geoff Lindsay and Martin Desforges
April 1998 and July 1999

Chapter 1

Baseline assessment: political background to educational change

Introduction

The frantic pace of educational change in the UK over the past decade can be traced back to the 1988 Education Reform Act, which in its preamble stated that the Act was to:

> promote the spiritual, moral, cultural, mental, and physical development of pupils and of society; and prepare pupils for the opportunities, responsibilities and experiences of adult life

There would be few who would disagree with such praiseworthy aims, but many who would question whether the structures set up by the Act would help schools to achieve them.

A central part of the legislation was the setting up of a National Curriculum and its associated framework of assessment. The structure of the National Curriculum described each subject area in terms of ten levels of attainment stating the knowledge and skills that defined each level. The years of compulsory education were divided into four key stages, and set levels of attainment that should be reached by the average pupil at the end of each key stage (see Table 1.1).

Table 1.1 National Curriculum assessment

Key Stage	Age range (years)	Average level attained at end of Key Stage
1	5–7	Level 2
2	7–11	Level 4
3	11–14	Levels 5–6
4	14–16	Levels 6–7

It also laid out a statutory framework for assessment at the end of each key stage, together with the requirement that results on an individual pupil basis must be given to parents, and results on an aggregated school and LEA basis must be published at the end of Key Stages 2 and 3, together with GCSE and A level results for secondary schools. In 1994 a review of the National Curriculum (Dearing 1994) recommended that assessment at the end of Key Stage 4 should not use the levels of the National Curriculum, but simply use GCSE grades.

The major stated aims were to raise educational standards, to improve the education of all children, and to increase the accountability of schools to the client groups they serve – defined as parents and industry, but not pupils or local communities. A further aim was to introduce market economics into education. There should be an element of choice for consumers, leading to competition between schools. This was thought to provide a healthy stimulus to improve quality, to the benefit of pupils, parents and the national economy. As in any period of rapid change, different parts of the political and educational system tried to influence the outcomes of these reforms, and the struggle between ministers, civil servants and educational professionals during the implementation of these reforms is documented by Graham and Tytler (1993).

Other reforms to curb the power of local government and reduce its role in education led to the setting up of grant maintained schools totally independent of the LEA, the local management of schools and delegation of both finance and decision making away from LEAs to individual schools. Changes to the composition of governing bodies, and extending their powers further reduced the role of the LEA. Alongside these changes were mechanisms to make schools more accountable to the communities they served – publishing of league tables of results of public examinations and end of key stage National Curriculum assessments, the regular inspection of schools by OFSTED and the publication of the resulting reports. A further thrust was the declared intention of central government that educational standards should be improved, and that schools would be held publicly accountable for their failures.

Educational standards

The concerns about educational standards seem to be perennial, and were as much part of earlier Labour administrations as they were of the Tory government between 1979 and 1997. The Labour Prime Minister James Callaghan in 1976 made a speech in Oxford where he declared that he wanted to start a great debate on education, and at the root of his concerns was a fear of declining educational standards, possibly sparked off by the moves to comprehensive schools at secondary level during the 1960s and early 1970s.

It is worth noting that the evidence to support these views of declining standards is tenuous, with ever increasing percentages of each age cohort obtaining five or more grade A–C at GCSE, and greater percentages going on to higher education as the annual statistics from the Department for Education and Employment show. The 1990–91 panic about falling reading standards in primary schools was set off by educational psychologists reporting results of authority-wide reading tests from a small number of LEAs. Subsequent investigations by HMI (1990) and NFER (Cato and Whetton 1991) could not find evidence to support these alarmist views, other than a small decrement in performance that appeared to coincide with the introduction of the National Curriculum. This led to a further dimension to the debate on falling standards, with comparisons being made with other countries world wide, particularly with the countries of the Pacific Rim, to demonstrate a relative decline in the levels of basic numeracy and literacy of UK pupils.

Richards (1997) notes that primary education has long been the subject of myth-making, and summarises the current negative myths as 'children are not being taught to read, write and calculate properly, they while away the day on trivial pursuits, and their standards of attainments are lower than their predecessors of twenty, thirty or forty years ago'. He is especially critical of the way OFSTED reports make use of their own data to paint a gloomy picture of primary education that is very difficult to substantiate, even from those data.

The new Labour administration which came to power in May 1997 seems to be pursuing similar policies to the previous government, based on the belief that standards of education are generally unsatisfactory in state schools. The priority given to education in the general election campaign was followed up two months later by the White Paper *Excellence in Schools* published in July 1997. An important belief in how school improvement can be brought about seems to be that

> given the right balance of pressure and support, standards rise fastest where schools take responsibility for their own improvement. (SCAA 1997a, p.1)

The School Curriculum and Assessment Authority (SCAA) had already indicated the importance of education in the early years if pupils were to make satisfactory progress in National Curriculum subjects during Key

Stage 1. *Desirable Outcomes for Children's Learning on Entering Compulsory Education* (SCAA 1996a) set out a pre-school curriculum focusing on six areas of learning: personal and social development, language and literacy, mathematics, knowledge and understanding of the world, physical development and creative development. The document describes in some detail how desirable outcomes in each of these areas contributes to National Curriculum targets in Key Stage 1. The major emphasis for the function of nursery education is on the preparation of pre-school children for the National Curriculum, rather than a balanced consideration of the child developmental perspective. The role of nursery education to support National Curriculum achievements is clearly expressed in *Excellence in Schools* (DfEE 1997a), which on page 17 states

> The 'outcomes' provide national standards for early years education . . . and are designed to provide a robust first step towards the National Curriculum and we shall re-examine them at the same time as we review the National Curriculum.

It would be hard to give a clearer statement of views on the function of nursery education.

Whilst the Desirable Outcomes document does not have a statutory basis, its publication coincided with legislation on the introduction of vouchers for pre-school education. As a condition of validation for the receipt of vouchers, institutions were required to publish a statement of the education provided. Confirmation of validation was based on a judgement, through inspection, about the extent to which the quality of provision is appropriate to the desirable outcomes in each area of learning. Although nursery vouchers have now been withdrawn, inspection of nursery provision based on the Desirable Outcomes document will continue, and SCAA has published guidance on good practice (SCAA 1997e).

National Curriculum assessment

A major theme in the development of the National Curriculum has been the central role of assessment, and the way results have been used for a variety of purposes. There are three major purposes of assessment: firstly to inform teachers and pupils of the progress being made and to decide the next steps in learning (formative); secondly for the certification of individual students to provide a publicly recognised standard that the student has achieved at the end of a particular stage of education (summative); and finally to provide information serving the public accountability of schools and teachers for their successes and failures (evaluative). This last function is the one that has received the most publicity in recent years with the publication of league tables of how successful schools are in terms of National Curriculum Key Stage 2, GCSE and A level results. The difficulties of making sense of this information is dealt with at length in Chapter 4.

So far, National Curriculum Key Stage 1 results have not formed part of published league tables, and there are still many uncertainties about the reliability and validity of all end of key stage National Curriculum assessments, as no information on their technical quality has been made available, despite the claim in *Excellence in Schools* that 'we now have sound, consistent, national measures of pupil achievement for each school at each key stage of the National Curriculum' (p.25). The thinking of the new Labour Government on the use of assessment information is clear. They have expressed the view that each school and LEA should set annual targets for improvement. A consultation paper *Target Setting and Benchmarking in Schools* was produced by SCAA in September 1997. There is the belief that parents and others should have raw results on attainments, and that this should be supplemented by a measure of how much progress individual pupils have made during each key stage. At the end of Key Stages 2 and 3 the results at the end of the previous key stage can be used to measure progress, but this is not possible for Key Stage 1 unless baseline assessment is introduced for all five year old pupils as they enter infant school.

Purposes of baseline assessment

Baseline assessment is now enshrined in law. The Education Act 1997 gave the starting date for compulsory baseline assessment of five year olds as September 1998, and despite the change of government, the Labour administration are committed to this timetable. They have declared that they want this to be the first form of assessment introduced on the basis of partnership with teachers, and not confrontation with them, and that it has a crucial role in the measurement of added-value:

> As baseline assessment at age 5 is progressively introduced, it will be possible to measure any pupil's progress through his or her school career, and also compare that pupil with any other individual or group, whether locally or nationally. (DfEE 1997a, p.25)

The historical roots of baseline assessment are in the early identification of special educational needs (SEN), going back more than 20 years. Before then, earlier systems, such as Child Guidance, attempted to provide a service which helped identify the developmental difficulties of children and young people, and then offer an intervention aimed at amelioration (Sampson 1980). Epidemiological studies pointed to the benefits of the systematic examination of whole cohorts of children to identify those with educational difficulties (Rutter *et al.* 1970), but these investigations were often later in children's educational careers, with an obvious delay before intervention could take place to help those with difficulties. In an effort to overcome these difficulties, a group of educational psychologists, education advisers and headteachers became interested in trying to identify children before they developed educational problems, that is, those 'at risk'. A number of psychologists developed approaches to aid the early identification of children who may be at risk of developing educational difficulties (Wolfendale and Bryans 1979, Lindsay 1981, Pearson and Quinn 1986).

Wolfendale (1993) notes that in the early 1990s baseline assessment was linked with a new set of purposes – a way of helping to impose practice in terms of early record keeping and profiling of children's attainments as they enter infant school to help curriculum planning, provide appropriate curriculum differentiation and ensure progression for each child. At the same time the Record of Achievement movement had been very successful at Secondary school level in broadening the base of assessment, and giving much greater importance both to self-assessment skills and to personal and social development as well as academic attainment (e.g. Broadfoot *et al.* 1989). These new approaches to assessment were taken up by primary schools, and schemes such as All About Me (Wolfendale 1990) and the Sheffield Primary Record of Achievement and Experience (Sheffield LEA 1993) were developed, to include the transition from home to infant school.

Baseline assessment was also linked to the National Curriculum, and its associated assessment procedures, that at Key Stages 2 and 3 had led to school league tables. Concern at the unfairness of average raw scores being used to judge school effectiveness, with little or no contextual information such as socio-economic factors of the catchment area or rate of progress made during the key stage, had led to the notion of 'value-added'. It was thought that the results at the end of the previous National Curriculum key stage could be used to calculate the value-added component of how effectively the school had taught the child. But what of Key Stage 1? Some headteachers, particularly of separate infant schools, or nursery and infant schools, had become interested in assessing developmental levels when children first entered school, and using this as a baseline against which progress could be measured at the end of Key Stage 1.

There were clear tensions between the broader base of the Records of Achievement approach to early assessment, and the school curriculum based approach of the National Curriculum, and it was difficult to see how these tensions could be resolved (Desforges 1991).

Lindsay (1998) considers the many purposes of baseline assessment, and groups them into two major categories, each with several different purposes.

Table 1.2 Purposes of baseline assessment

Child focus	School focus
Early identification of pupils with SEN	Resource planning
Early identification of pupil's SEN	Accountability: value-added
Monitoring progress of all pupils	Budget determination
Identify learning objectives and teaching strategies for individual pupils	School improvement

Child focus

Early identification of children with SEN. If we are to identify individual children with SEN, *all* children must be screened, followed by a further assessment phase for all those identified as possibly at risk on the screening measure. Many teachers are concerned about the dangers of early labelling five-year-old pupils in what they see as a negative way, but recognise the benefits if it leads to positive outcomes for the children identified.

Early identification of children's SEN. To identify the specific difficulties and resulting educational needs of particular children, there is a need for a more detailed examination of the child's profile using either, or both, normative and criterion referenced measures. Such assessments may be carried out by other support workers as well as the class teacher or Special Educational Needs Coordinator (SENCO).

Monitoring all children's progress. There is now a better understanding of the need to monitor the progress of all children, not just those with special educational needs, to ensure progress and to allow differentiation to provide an appropriate curriculum if learning is not happening.

Identification of teaching goals and steps to learning. The final purpose of child focused assessment is to specify learning objectives and teaching strategies. This must take account of the child's need for a broad and balanced curriculum as well as specific curricular needs in the basic subjects, even though the requirements on schools to follow programmes of study in the six non-core basic subjects have been relaxed (OFSTED 1998b).

School focus

The second set of purposes for baseline assessment are concerned with the school's response to the needs of its pupils, and its accountability to its community.

Resource planning. Firstly, the school must make decisions about the needs of their clientele in order to plan the teaching and resourcing programme. This is essentially an internal affair with decisions made within the school by senior management and the governors.

Accountability and value-added. The school must be accountable in terms of its learning outcomes, and baseline assessment contributes to an analysis of value-added. This could be a completely internal affair. The new benchmark information (PANDAs) which were distributed to schools in the Spring of 1998 allow comparisons between the school and those judged similar. Hence outcome measures such as end of key stage assessments may be compared. In addition, baseline assessment may contribute to value-added analyses which are intended to allow any school to judge the pupils' progress, as opposed to their absolute levels of attainment. Again, these rates of progress could be compared with those of similar schools once such data are available, so allowing judgements of relative rates of progress, the assumption being that different rates are attributable to school factors. However, these outcomes are now required to be publicised rather than be used only internally to the school.

Budget determination. Baseline assessment may provide data to aid LEAs allocate finance through the Local Management of Schools (LMS) school budget formula, required under Section 122 of the Education Act

1996. This is relatively new. Most LEAs have used entitlement to free school meals as a proxy measure for estimating an SEN element in the formula. This has a reasonable rationale, as free school meals entitlement is correlated with social disadvantage, which in turn is correlated with lower achievement and higher levels of disaffection and behaviour problems (e.g. Essen and Wedge 1982). However, some LEAs have preferred to use test results on entry or audits of SEN as an attempt at a more direct assessment of need for the purpose of budget allocation. Such audits and testings have generally been of older children. Sheffield is one LEA which has pioneered the use of baseline assessment for this purpose for infant schools and departments.

School improvement. The final purpose is that of school improvement. This also is essentially a within-school matter. The analyses described under 'Accountability and value-added' may be used for action. Given the comparisons, a school may decide that, for example, its literacy scores are below a reasonable expectation. Baseline assessment may provide the information on the school's intake to allow a judgement of what is a reasonable goal for improvement, or series of goals over, say, a five year period.

The SCAA proposals for baseline assessment

Baseline assessment is now a legal requirement under the Education Act 1997 Part 4 Chapter 1 which states:

> 'baseline assessment scheme' means a scheme designed to enable pupils at a maintained primary school to be assessed for the purpose of assisting the future planning of their education and the measurement of their future educational achievement.

Interestingly the majority of the guidance for implementation was already in place before the legislation was on the statute book. In this section we shall trace this development.

The Government's intentions with respect to baseline assessment have been implemented by the School Curriculum and Assessment Authority (SCAA), now the Qualifications and Curriculum Authority (QCA). These proposals have been developed through a process of conducting surveys of opinion, the production and trialling of three different models of baseline assessment, followed by an evaluation of the SCAA scheme (SCAA 1996c, 1996d, 1997c, Caspall *et al.* 1997). Arising from this work,

9

draft proposals for the implementation of baseline assessment for five year olds were published in September 1996 (SCAA 1996b). The report concludes that the consultation process provided consensus that 'the primary purpose of baseline assessment schemes should be to provide formative and diagnostic information to the teacher' (p.6). The report goes on to list seven purposes to achieve its aim, five of which are concerned with the individual child (e.g. to identify the child's strengths and learning needs) and clearly fit the primary purpose stated above. However two other stated aims, one to form part of a value-added measure, and one to aid accountability do not.

Later, in proposal 10 of the draft document, SCAA argue that all schemes of baseline assessment should measure children's progress in a consistent way, for potential use as a value-added measurement. Although the consultation exercise described above showed that teachers saw baseline assessment primarily as identifying the strengths and learning needs of children, and to help teachers plan effectively, the use of baseline assessment for value-added purposes has been given prominence by SCAA.

The draft proposals were subject to a round of consultation while the three schemes were being evaluated. There was support for a national framework rather than one national scheme, and for baseline assessment being compulsory. The final report (SCAA 1997c) notes that the use of baseline assessment for value-added 'generated much discussion' but 'overall there was strong support for it' (p.2). However, 'there was some debate about the extent to which the two purposes for baseline assessment can be met through one assessment instrument' (p.2). Indeed, the consensus wanted a great deal from baseline assessment:

> There was widespread agreement that baseline assessment could be used to identify children's strengths and learning needs, enable teachers to plan appropriately, identify children with special educational needs, assist curriculum and resource planning, form part of a value-added measure and aid accountability. (SCAA 1997c, p.3)

There were three areas of concern: that a national scheme might be imposed, that outcomes be used to generate performance tables, and that successful implementation would require considerable resources.

The final document on implementing baseline assessment, *The National Framework for Baseline Assessment* (SCAA 1997d), was published in June 1997, confirming that there would be a national framework rather than a single scheme developed by SCAA. The model is one of setting quality standards, and then allowing various methods to achieve the agreed objectives, to those standards. There was also an allocation of £8.5 million from the GEST funding scheme for the 1997–98 financial year to support the introduction of baseline assessment.

This document sets out the purposes of baseline assessment and the criteria and procedures for the accreditation of baseline assessment schemes (SCAA 1997d). The key principles and requirements are shown in Figure 1.1.

The key principles are divided into two categories and arise from the proposals already outlined. The first category identifies the essential principles required of all baseline assessment schemes. The second category identifies additional principles which the National Framework would encourage as features of good practice.

The National Framework will require baseline assessment schemes to:

- ensure equal entitlement for all children to be assessed, including those children for whom English is an additional language;
- be sufficiently detailed to identify individual children's learning needs, including special educational needs, in order to support effective and appropriate planning for teaching and learning;
- enable children's later progress to be monitored effectively;
- involve parents/carers in partnership with the school;
- take place in the first half term of the child's entry to the reception class (or year one if the child enters school at that point);
- focus as a minimum on early literacy and numeracy;
- be unobtrusive for children;
- be manageable for teachers; and
- provide outcomes which will contribute to value-added measurement.

The National Framework will encourage baseline assessment schemes to:

- contribute to the child's attainment record over the key stage;
- build upon assessments and records from pre-school providers;
- include accounts of
  - personal and social development
  - physical development
  - creative development
  - other aspects of children's development, e.g. knowledge and understanding of the world;
- be an integral part of the school's assessment policy.

Figure 1.1 Key principles of the national framework (SCAA 1996d, p.12)

From September 1998 all maintained primary schools in England will be required to use a baseline assessment scheme for all entrants to infant school, and the scheme must be accredited by QCA. The document states that baseline assessment has two key purposes:

- to provide information to help teachers plan effectively to meet children's individual learning needs;
- to measure children's attainment, using one or more numerical outcomes which can be used in later value-added analyses of children's progress.

The document goes on to give detailed guidance on criteria for getting schemes accredited, and the information which must be provided, as set out in Figure 1.2.

Requirements for baseline assessment schemes

Baseline assessment schemes must specify how the assessment of children is to be carried out. They must provide an equal entitlement for all children to be assessed on entry to school. Schemes must:

- cover aspects of language and literacy, mathematics, and personal and social development as specified in the *Desirable Outcomes for Children's Learning on Entering Compulsory Education;*
- include clear guidance to teachers on how the outcomes of the assessment can be used to inform the planning both for a class and for individual children;
- provide one or more numerical outcomes capable of being used for later value-added analysis; and
- specify the period after a child has started at primary school within which an assessment should be completed. This period should, in normal circumstances, be no longer than seven weeks after a child has started primary school.

Requirements for scheme providers

A scheme provider must include clear guidance for administering its scheme. The nature and length of guidance in these areas is up to the scheme provider.

A scheme provider must demonstrate:

- the manageability of the scheme by specifying how long teachers should expect it to take them to administer the scheme.

Figure 1.2 Accreditation criteria (*The National Framework for Baseline Assessment*, SCAA 1997d, pp.6–7)

A scheme provider must include guidance on procedures for:

- how teachers can use records of children's pre-school experience, where these are available, to inform the assessment of their attainment and to help plan for their further learning;
- how teachers should assess the attainment of children for whom English is an additional language;
- how the scheme links to more detailed assessments which identify children's special educational needs and more able children;
- recording the numerical outcomes of the assessment in a form that aids the analysis of the outcomes; and
- explaining the outcomes of assessments to parents. As a minimum, this should include the opportunity for a discussion between parents and their child's teacher within a term of the child being admitted to the school.

The scheme provider must also provide details of:

- the data which would normally be collected on each child;
- how it proposes to collect data from schools;
- the analyses which will be provided to schools registered with the scheme;
- the training which it considers necessary for schools taking up its scheme; and
- its planned procedures for ensuring the quality and consistency of assessments carried out as part of its scheme.

The scheme provider will also be required:

- to keep a register of schools using its scheme;
- to make available to any LEA the list of schools registered with its scheme, which the LEA maintains; and
- to make an annual return to SCAA/QCA of the schools registered as using its scheme.

Figure 1.2 (continued)

The schemes must cover, as a basic minimum, aspects of language and literacy, mathematics and personal and social development as specified in the *Desirable Outcomes for Children's Learning on Entering Compulsory Education* (SCAA 1996a). It is interesting to note that the basic minimum is only three of the six areas specified in the Desirable Outcomes document, reinforcing the view that teaching and learning will follow testing in focusing on aspects that are easy (or easier) to assess, rather than on what is important (Black 1996). Although schemes can cover a wider range of areas than the three listed above, the document stresses the need for demands on teacher time to be realistic and manageable. If schemes involve assessments that mean the teacher cannot teach the rest of the class, the maximum time should not exceed 20 minutes per child.

A scheme must provide one or more numerical outcomes capable of being used for later value-added analysis, and specify the period after a child has started primary school within which an assessment should be completed. This should normally be no longer than seven weeks after primary school entry. It must also include clear guidance to teachers on how the outcomes of assessment can be used to inform planning both for a class and for individual children.

The headteacher of each primary school has the responsibility of selecting a scheme from the list of accredited baseline assessment schemes, and recommending the scheme to the governing body to consider for formal adoption. In making this selection the headteacher must consider first the scheme nominated by their own LEA. Although LEAs are not required to provide their own scheme, they must nominate an accredited scheme for recommendation to schools in the LEA. This may be a scheme it has developed itself, or a scheme developed elsewhere that has been accredited by QCA. Headteachers have the power to exempt individual children from baseline assessment if in their judgement such an assessment would be inappropriate (e.g. where a child is at Stage 4 of the SEN Code of Practice). Headteachers will also have the power to modify assessments where in their judgement this is appropriate for particular children

The document suggests that much useful information about children can be gained by teachers in primary schools from pre-school providers, and that records should be used to learn more about pupils' attainments before the child starts school, or no later than the first two weeks of starting primary school. The guidance on pupils' speaking English as an additional language states that teachers must assess children's attainments in speaking, listening, reading and writing to establish their fluency in English. However, English, the child's preferred language, or both, may be used to assess attainments in mathematics, personal and social development and any other areas covered by the scheme.

Baseline assessment needs to link with the more detailed assessment of children with special educational needs as prescribed by the Code of Practice (DfE 1994). The baseline assessment should be helpful in the early identification of children with learning difficulties, and can lead on to a more detailed and diagnostic assessment of their teaching and learning needs.

Guidance for schools states that the results of baseline assessment must be shared with parents, and that sometime during the first term all parents are offered the opportunity of a discussion with their child's teacher about the outcomes of baseline assessment. Before this meeting schools may choose to provide parents with a written report or record of the outcome of baseline assessment.

Finally, the scheme must provide analyses of performance data for each school for all children assessed using the scheme, for boys and girls separately, and for month of birth. Analyses of data to provide comparative data for each school using the scheme, or for groupings related to factors such as pre-school provision, ethnicity or community language are optional.

Surprisingly, no reference whatsoever is made to any requirements regarding the technical quality of the schemes themselves. There is no mention of a scheme needing to provide data on its reliability or validity. The criteria mention the issue of quality assurance, stating that scheme providers are responsible for giving details of proposed procedures for securing quality and consistency of assessments. They suggest these may include a combination of training for teachers in conducting assessments in a standard way, moderation meetings for teachers to discuss interpretation of children's performance, or visits to schools by representatives of scheme providers. However, they do not require data to support the effectiveness of these suggested measures.

Desforges and Lindsay (1995b) note that over the last twenty years many LEAs have decided to develop programmes for early identification of educational difficulties for use in the first year of primary school. These projects were often limited to developing an instrument for an agreed purpose, with little in the way of evaluative research to look at issues of reliability, validity and fitness for purpose. It is as though the belief that the views of those professionals concerned is sufficient to develop an appropriate checklist or screening device. If major decisions are made on the outcomes of such assessments, and the instruments are of less than satisfactory quality, significant errors may arise, possibly contributing to harmful outcomes for children and for schools.

The criterion for there to be numerical outcomes states that these should be capable of being used for later value-added analysis. There is no guidance as to whether this should be a composite score including performance in the three core areas of language and literacy, mathematics and personal and social development, or whether a numerical outcome from any one of these areas alone will be sufficient. Given that schools and scheme providers may chose to use different aspects of the data for use in arriving at the value-added factor, how can schools be compared? We return to this issue in more detail in Chapter 4.

Concerns over baseline assessment

While interest in standards and a national assessment system is common in many countries, interest in baseline assessment is less common (Wilkinson and Napuk 1997). Also, where a well developed scheme is in operation, it may not have the same range of aims as that being developed in England and Wales. For example, the New Zealand scheme, introduced into all primary schools in 1997, is concerned with providing information about each new entrant to school, assisting decision making by the school with regard to resources, and contributing to national policy development and allocation of resources: value-added analyses are notably absent (Wilkinson and Napuk 1997). However, the scheme in Northern Ireland appears to be following that in England and Wales.

Concerns over baseline assessment cover a broad range, with theoretical, ideological, practical and financial dimensions. Wolfendale (1993) summarises some of these and asks whether baseline assessment will lead to a narrowing of the curriculum, with teachers concentrating on what is assessed rather than what is important. Will teacher expectations be set by the results of baseline assessment, leading to the early labelling of children? Can one instrument fulfil several different purposes (formative, used for allocating resources, as a basis for value-added, identification of special educational needs)? How do we ensure baseline assessment does not reduce the educational opportunities of children from a minority ethnic background?

Others have questioned the possibility of baseline assessment at any level, and appear to reject the view that different types of assessment can be appropriate for different purposes. Drummond (1993) dismisses baseline assessment as 'dead end assessment', believing it ludicrous that such schedules can embody 'any respect for children's minds, for their powers to think, to create, to imagine, to explore, to reason, to puzzle, to wonder, to dream'. The notion of assessments fit for a particular purpose, even if they do not presume to measure the higher order cognitive skills set out by Drummond, appears to be rejected.

Nutbrown (1997) accepts the notion that different assessments will be needed for different purposes, and states that assessments designed to inform teaching and learning of individual children will not be the same as instruments needed for value-added. However she then goes on to say that efforts put into entry assessments must be in the interests of children and their learning *at the time of assessment* (her emphasis), seemingly rejecting any justification of assessments that may be in the future interests of the child. Blatchford and Cline (1992) set out a scheme for evaluating baseline assessment, which seems to assume that a multiplicity of purposes must be served by any instrument, rather than focusing on fitness for purpose.

Attempts to address a variety of purposes are usually fraught with dangers, and this is the case with baseline assessment. Shaping up a procedure to enhance its strength in one area is likely to lead to problems in other domains. As we shall show, there are inherent conflicts in using a baseline assessment for identifying children's learning needs in the present and as a measure against which to plot later achievement to determine the relative value-added by the school. The decision to allow a large number of schemes has positive aspects, but does remove the possibility of any valid comparison of value-added nationally, which seems a curious confusion of aims and operations

All these issues will be considered in the chapters that follow, as we try to differentiate the purposes, processes and policies which drive or follow from baseline assessment. Throughout the book you will be presented with information that will help you reach your own conclusions on the possibilities, and the limitations, of baseline assessment

Chapter 2

Child development

Introduction

Development involves change over time, with both parents and teachers having some expectations of what constitutes normal development, and what stage of development is associated with particular age groups – two-year-old tantrums, the fantasy world of the six-year-old and the truculent teenager are some of the more familiar stages. The models of child development that we carry in our heads usually cover many different aspects of development: biological, psychological and social.

The main themes in development include, firstly, the biological notion of increasing size from infancy to adulthood, secondly, the acquisition of a variety of skills – walking, fine motor control, language, thinking skills, social skills – and, thirdly, the integration of these individual skills into complex patterns of automatic, high-level performance where we can carry out several tasks simultaneously without having consciously to think about each aspect of the many tasks involved.

Psychological theories of development tend to present a picture of a systematic progression through a series of stages common to all children, leading to maturity, where earlier patterns of behaviour are replaced by more sophisticated forms. As Rutter and Rutter (1992) point out, these theories emphasise the universals of development rather than the individual differences, and each tends to focus on only one aspect of development.

Piaget (1953) focused on stages of cognitive development from the sensori-motor stage of early infancy, through the pre-operational and concrete operational stages of childhood to the formal operations of adolescence and adulthood. Bowlby (1969) put forward a theory of attachment between infant and caregivers that had profound influences on our understanding of anxiety, learning, exploratory and social behaviour. Gesell (1946) described development in terms of milestones in the areas of physical, motor, and perceptual development, suggesting not just a fixed sequence of development, but also the ages associated with each milestone. Erikson (1968) looked at social aspects of development, with his stages focusing on those age-related social tasks and the skills that each child needed to acquire before they could move to the next stage.

There are a number of criticisms of these stage theories of human development. Each concentrates on a particular aspect of development, and fails to show how that aspect integrates with, and both influences and is influenced by, other aspects of development. Most tend to assume a certain inevitability, described by Rutter and Rutter (1992) as

> a mechanical predictability out of keeping with the dynamics of change, the extent of flux over time, and the degree of individual variability. (p.2)

This predictability suggests that there is just one developmental path that we each tread, leading to an end-point called maturity reached in late adolescence or early adulthood. A very different perspective is one of life itself being a developmental process which ends only with death. Throughout our lives we are on a journey of change where we learn new skills, establish new relationships and our experiences cause us to change our views of the world and of life itself.

The second criticism concerns the notion of stages itself. Is this a convenient metaphor to indicate rapid rates of change at certain times, or does each stage represent a significant break with previous ways of functioning? In terms of cognitive development, Donaldson and her co-workers (Donaldson 1978) have built up a considerable body of experimental work which undermines Piaget's stages of cognitive development, and suggests rather more continuities in terms of how children's thinking develops, first deeply embedded in personal experiences and the social context in which they live, to a perspective where logical thought becomes less dependent on context and moves to more abstract forms.

Stage theories tend to assume that as we move from one stage to the next, the earlier mode of functioning drops from the repertoire. Whilst this may be true for some aspects of cognitive development, social and emotional development is best construed as an increasing repertoire of reactions and behaviours that we can call upon in any one situation. Although we talk about two-year-old temper tantrums, many older children and some adults will use this behaviour pattern in their intimate personal relationships. The range of emotions and behaviours we show is dependent on where we are and who we are with. Extremes of anger, sadness or happiness are more likely to occur in private with those we share a close relationship – parents, partners, siblings or offspring – than with work colleagues or managers.

Despite these criticisms, most of these stage theories accept the subtle interplay between genetic factors and environmental influences (both biological and social) in the finer details of development, and many postulate sensitive periods of learning, with biologically determined windows of time where optimal learning is possible. If appropriate stimulation is not received during this window of opportunity, there may be long-lasting consequences. However, the major feature of all these theories is the orderliness, predictability and continuities in the developmental process.

The concept of continuity is important because it informs the notion of baseline assessment and the possibility of measuring value-added. It is assumed that because a particular individual is performing at the well above average level at one point in development, they will be expected to be doing equally well in the future. This was the justification for the eleven plus assessment which decided which pupils should go to grammar school, and which to technical and secondary modern schools. The top 15 to 20 per cent selected at age 11 were assumed to be the same individuals that would be expected to be performing at similar levels at age 16 and 18, and would hence benefit from an academic education. Similar thinking lies behind the use of baseline assessment at five to use in measuring value-added at the end of Key Stages 1 or 2.

Now clearly things are not that simple, and, for a variety of reasons, one might expect environmental factors to cause some changes in developmental status relative to peers over a period of years. However, the developmental process itself might be uneven, with differential rates of development between individuals across any time period. If this is the case one would expect quite marked changes in developmental status relative to peers even when environmental factors stay constant over a period of time. It is to this that we turn next.

Continuities and discontinuities in development

Let us consider a few examples. Body weight, length and head circumference are routinely measured at birth and at frequent intervals during the early years. Norm referenced charts are available so that the weight, height and head circumference of each individual can be compared with the distribution of these measures in the wider population. It is then possible to check whether growth patterns are following a normal trajectory. The assumption is that current measures are good predictors of future status, and any marked slowing down or acceleration of growth might be a cause of concern and a reason for further medical checks. Is a marked change in rate of weight increase a sign of illness, a metabolic disorder or a less than adequate feeding regime? Is a change in relative status of head circumference, from say the 45 centile to the 90 centile an indication of developing hydrocephalus? Or are these changes in status relative to the wider population simply caused by individuals having very different growth patterns with spurts and plateaus occurring at different times in different individuals. If this is the case, marked changes would be common, and not necessarily a cause of concern. If developmental processes are commonly of this irregular pattern there are clearly problems with long-term predictions based on a measure at one moment in time.

The picture is further complicated if we consider the possibility of sensitive periods of learning, where less than optimal stimulation during the sensitive period could have significant long-term consequences. Verbal language is a uniquely human attribute, and current thinking suggests a firm genetic base for its development. However, without the appropriate linguistic input at each stage of development, provided by caregivers and others forming the social milieu of the child, normal language development will not occur. Locke (1997) suggests four stages in the development of language:

Stage 1 – affective, where the infant orientates to the human face and learns the caregiver's vocal characteristics.

Stage 2 – affective and social, where the infant begins to learn words and phrases and the appropriate social context in which to use them. This is thought to be primarily controlled by the right hemisphere of the brain.

Stage 3 – analytical and computational, where the stored words and phrases are decomposed into syllables and segments, and the detection of regularities leading to classification with the discovery and application of grammar rules. This involves linguistic features such as syntax, morphology and phonology, and is thought to be primarily carried out by particular areas in the left side of the brain genetically pre-programmed for this function.

Stage 4 is integrative and elaborative, with further acquisition of words, syllables enabling extensive lexical learning and the use of more

21

sophisticated language structures and an increasing awareness of the rules governing the different social contexts in which language is used.

Locke feels that there is good evidence for sensitive periods of learning for each of these stages, but especially for stage 3. If the appropriate linguistic stimulation and subsequent learning have not occurred difficulties will arise. Children delayed at stage 2 will have too few stored words to trigger the analytical mechanism at stage 3 at the optimal biological moment, and by the time they have learned sufficient words, the capability of the brain structures involved will be in decline and therefore no longer capable of carrying out the task for which they were designed. Although alternative parts of the brain can take over some of these tasks, they are not as efficient. There is evidence that phonological skills, important at a later stage of development for learning to read and write, might be particularly affected. The effects may not show immediately in oral aspects of language, but only when the child is exposed to print.

It is not clear that failure to develop language at the normal stage necessarily means the child will never do so. Evidence from studies of children found to have been suffering severe deprivation throughout their early years show that where appropriate stimulation follows discovery before adolescence, a good recovery to normal adulthood is possible (Dockrell and Messer, in press). On the other hand, it is clear that delayed inputs or delayed learning at one stage of development may lead to difficulties at a later stage, with important consequences for school-based learning. Because the symptoms at the time may be minimal and hard to detect, it illustrates the difficulties of predicting future problems on the basis of information gathered at an earlier stage of development.

Another theory suggesting sensitive periods of learning with long-term consequences if things go wrong at an early stage is Bowlby's theory of Attachment (see Bowlby 1969). He placed great importance on the early infant–caregiver bonding process, with predicted long-term negative consequences for anxiety, learning and interpersonal relationships if this bonding process was disrupted during the first 12 to 24 months of life. Although many aspects of his theory were accepted, and had profound effects on social policy relating to childcare, fostering and adoption, and hospital treatment of young children, it is now clear that the long-term consequences of separation are not necessarily as severe as Bowlby's work first suggested (see Rutter 1981).

Longitudinal studies of development

Despite our recognition and understanding of the subtle complexities of the many factors influencing the developmental process at different levels – biological, psychological and social – we continue to have difficulties in understanding cause and effect relationships in human development, and have limited success in predicting developmental pathways rather than trying retrospectively to reconstruct the significant factors that lead an individual to their present situation. When we look at longitudinal studies we are struck by the unevenness and unpredictability of the developmental process.

This point is illustrated by a number of studies looking at changes in IQ scores over time. Hindley and Owen (1978) looked at variations in IQ scores of a group of children from infancy to late adolescence. Between the ages of five and 11, 25 per cent were found to have changed by 16 IQ points, and three per cent by 30 or more points. Between the ages of 11 and 17 years, 25 per cent had changed by more than 19 points. An examination of individual profiles over the period of study showed that the predominant pattern was of irregular increases and decreases.

Moffitt *et al.* (1993) carried out a similar study over a seven year period on nearly 800 New Zealand children, giving the Wechsler Intelligence Scale for Children (Revised) at two-yearly intervals from age seven to age 13. An analysis of the individual profiles showed that for the majority the changes over time were negligible in amount and appeared to be random fluctuations, test error, or both. However, some 15 per cent showed significant but irregular fluctuations around a central point rather than a steady decline or improvement over the seven years. They were unable to identify any environmental factors correlated with the changes, and concluded that it was not possible to predict which children's performance would be subject to fluctuations over time.

In a study of psychiatric disorders, Esser *at al.* (1990) came to similar conclusions. They carried out a longitudinal study of children from age eight to age 13, and found that of the individuals with psychiatric disorders at the age of eight, only half still exhibited such disorders at 13, and many who showed disorders at 13 showed no signs at age eight. Again it was not possible to predict which individuals showing psychiatric disorders at the age of eight would continue with the symptoms at 13, and which would have recovered.

Clarke and Clarke (1985) suggest four factors influencing the pattern of individual development. Firstly, there are biological factors which have a varying influence on different psychological processes at different periods

23

of development. Secondly, there are social factors of family, friends, school and community. Thirdly, there are interactional processes, which acknowledge the fact that individuals are not just passive recipients of the various forces which impinge on their lives, but react to them as well as being influenced by them. Finally there are chance factors which can play a small or large part in influencing development – illness, disease, accidents, chance meetings with influential or charismatic individuals. All this adds up to what Clarke and Clarke call the *principle of developmental uncertainty*.

The prediction of developmental pathways is difficult, and finding causal relationships problematic. A common finding from longitudinal research projects into human development is that correlations decrease progressively as the interval between assessments increases. This may be due to reliability factors in the assessment method, fluctuations in scores as a result of variations in motivation, concentration and alertness. It may also reflect genuine changes in the relative status of the individual compared with the wider population.

Predicting educational attainments

The same problems hold true with predicting educational attainments. Reading readiness tests and profiles given either just before or at school entry proved to have limited prognostic value in terms of picking out those individuals who will later have difficulties with literacy skill development (Lindsay and Wedell 1982). Wells and Raban (1978) in a longitudinal study found that pre-school children's concepts about print and letter-name knowledge were related to reading attainments when tested at the age of seven using the Neale Comprehension test. Letter identification pre-school correlated with the reading test about 0.69, concepts about print at 0.62. The English Picture Vocabulary test given pre-school was found to correlate about 0.4 with the reading test given at the age of seven.

Blatchford *et al.* (1987) investigated how well children performed on six aspects of pre-school reading and followed them up by administering Young's reading test at seven years of age. The results for five measures (word reading scale was found to be too difficult) are shown in Table 2.1. All are statistically significant, but no one factor accounted for more than 35–40 per cent of the variance, with letter identification showing the highest correlation.

Stuart (1995) carried out a longitudinal study to compare two different screening batteries used in the first term of Infant schooling to identify

24

children at risk of having difficulties learning to read. The children's reading attainments were then tested at the end of their first year of infant school using the British Ability Scales (BAS) Word Reading Test. One screening battery was an adaptation of the Clay battery used in her Reading Recovery programme, the other was a test of phonological awareness and knowledge of sound-to-letter (PASCL). Both batteries were significantly correlated with the word reading score, Clay battery at 0.8, PASCL at 0.73.

Table 2.1 Predictors of reading at seven years of age

Reading skill	Correlation with Young's reading test
Word matching	0.31
Concepts about print	0.27
Letter identification	0.61
WPPSI vocabulary	0.36
Handwriting skills	0.49

Lazo and Pumfrey (1996) report similar links between tasks assessing phonological awareness pre-school and reading at age seven. They found that rhyme identity, alliteration identity, onset-rime isolation all correlated positively with scores on the BAS Word Reading, but did not report details of the size of correlation.

All these studies indicate a positive relationship between variables measured at pre-school or at school entry and reading attainments at six years or seven years of age. But while they present correlations for *groups* of children, none look at the accuracy with which *individual* progress can be measured, particularly at how well they pick out those children who later have difficulties with reading.

Variations in rates and patterns of development

The difficulties with prediction may not only be an indication of shortcomings in the assessment instruments used; they may be telling us something of fundamental importance about the development process itself. Rates and patterns of development within any one individual may vary, and there may be important differences between individuals. Some will have smooth trajectories, showing very even rates across different ages, whereas others may be very variable, at one age well behind most of their peers, but then go through a phase of accelerated development, being well above average, before falling back to the average range. A further factor may be differences not only in rates of learning at different times, but in different strategies. Learning skilled tasks is often assumed to involve linear sequential hierarchies which are the same for most individuals. This model of learning lends itself to assessment at inter-mediate stages to discover how far an individual has reached in their progress to the end point. An alternative model would be to consider learning as a network, involving many alternative pathways, with a variety of starting points depending on strengths and weaknesses of pre-existing skills and attainments, as well as individual interests and motivations. This model makes assessments comparing relative progress of different individuals more difficult, as well as making it more difficult to use just one assessment instrument to measure baseline skills. Many of the factors causing such individual variation may be genetic, which interact with environmental factors to cause even greater differences between individuals.

An important assumption in many models of development emphasising continuities across time is that environmental variables will remain constant for any one individual. In a stable society with little change this might be true for socio-economic variables, although illness and bereavement within the family may still have effects on school-based learning and of course illness and bereavement may occur at different rates and in different ways in different socio-economic groups. For example, the probability of a child dying is twice as common in social class V than class I (Spencer 1996).

However, social and economic trends in the UK over the last twenty years have led to increasing social fragmentation, with an ever widening gap between rich and poor, and unemployment rates rising significantly. A rapid increase in home ownership has meant that job loss is often accompanied by an inability to pay the mortgage and a move of house under stressful circumstances. In these situations parents may be unable to meet the social and emotional needs of their children, leading to emotional and educational difficulties.

Even if alternative employment is found, the collapse of traditional industries such as coal and shipbuilding, mechanisation in iron and steel as well as other manufacturing industries, means a more mobile workforce. Increased mobility can lead to the disruption of support networks, with children and families more isolated and more vulnerable to stress factors.

Marital separation and divorce have increased over the same period.

Emotional and educational difficulties are not an inevitable consequence of parental separation and divorce, and the outcomes are largely dependent on how the separation is managed, but the research evidence suggests that the majority of children whose parents divorce are adversely affected and do have poorer educational outcomes than those whose parents stay together (Desforges 1995).

All these are somewhat random events, and likely to cause variations in educational attainments. They are further factors in trying to predict educational outcomes on the basis of earlier measures.

Compensatory interaction

The process of development is itself concerned with change, and it is unlikely that a pattern will be set in early life and continue unchanged through infancy and childhood into adolescence and adulthood. Discontinuities, as well as some continuities are to be expected (see Rutter and Rutter 1992). Current ideas and models of development attempt to reflect these complexities, taking into account the way various stress and support factors impinge on the life of an individual, and looking at how these may interact at particular times during development to protect an individual from life's vicissitudes, or to make them especially vulnerable (see Figure 2.1).

In this model, school and home are each seen as the focus of several potentially positive and negative influences, the former being supportive, the latter being stressors. There are also socio-economic factors including poverty and nutrition which are known to correlate with children's developmental progress. Thirdly there are factors intrinsic to the child. These may be biological (e.g. genetic endowment, damage to the central nervous system (CNS) owing to certain diseases such as rubella). They may also be noted as the behavioural manifestations themselves, memory deficits and impaired ability to process abstract information, for example. In this model, SEN may result from any of these types of influence.

A model which takes account of these factors was developed by Klaus Wedell and termed compensatory interaction (Wedell 1978, Wedell and Lindsay 1980). Children's status is conceptualised as the result of an interaction between their own intrinsic strengths and weaknesses, and those in their environment. This interaction may change over time. A simple version of this model is presented in Figure 2.2. Each dimension is in reality a continuum. Also, the environment is a series of environments including the classroom, school, family and community, and to a large extent these may be seen as nesting one within the other, as argued by Bronfenbrenner (1979). For example, there is the immediate learning environment of the child in a group, nested within the classroom. This in turn nests within the school, neighbourhood and society as a whole.

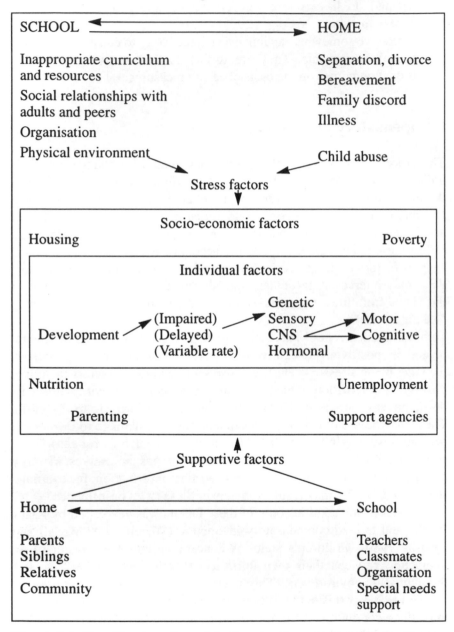

Figure 2.1 Identification of special educational needs: contributory factors

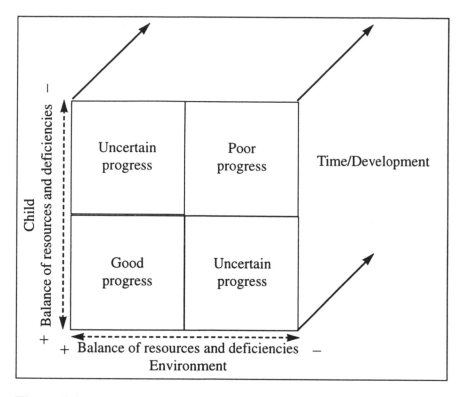

Figure 2.2 A model of compensatory interaction (Wedell and Lindsay 1980)

A child's personal resources may be positive (e.g. enthusiasm, fast processing of information) or negative (e.g. a hearing impairment, unhappiness, poor peer acceptance). At any one time these personal resources will be in some form of equilibrium, and with the resources from the different levels of the environment.

In this model, the child's abilities are not fixed and neither is performance. There might be dramatic variations in performance as a result of internal factors (e.g. a child with high distractibility or whose emotional life is in turmoil). Equally, the peer group, a change of teacher, or even higher level changes such as the introduction of the National Curriculum or an OFSTED inspection might impinge. As a result, measurement of performance over time highlights discontinuities as well as continuities, depending upon the overall interaction of these factors.

The likely outcomes, but note those are expressed as probabilities not certainties, are shown in Figure 2.2. This analysis might be taken further and used to characterise different types of learning difficulty, for example.

In Chapter 8 we discuss evidence on the effectiveness of interventions, where it will be seen that reading problems, for example, may not be caused by a reading disability as such, but rather by the inappropriateness of teaching.

The cause of a literacy problem, in this case, might be considered with reference to the model just described. Is there a basic problem with phonological processing (within the child); or is it due to the quality of teaching (see for example the latest report of Her Majesty's Chief Inspector, OFSTED (1998b)); or perhaps the curriculum, specified centrally by government through its agencies is the major cause? Again, as a model of probabilities, each element will have a part to play, but the overall balance of influence might vary from child to child. It is also the case that each may represent either a single, dominant influence, or two or more factors of relatively low impact individually may interact to produce a more substantial effect.

Returning to our model of compensatory interaction (Figure 2.2), the different influences will combine positively and negatively. Hence, while for a child with a degree of hearing loss teacher A aggravates his learning difficulties by her approach, teacher B helps to overcome these by her sensitivity and positive strategies.

This approach has important implications for our conceptualisation of special educational needs and for baseline assessment. Special educational needs are no longer seen as 'within the child' but rather as a result of this process of interaction. Users of baseline assessment cannot assume that these measures at age five years can identify children who 'have' SEN. Rather, the results can usefully point to SEN arising from the interaction between the child and the environment. Value-added analyses cannot legitimately be built upon an assumption that the child's status assessed at five years captures completely the 'within child' characteristics such that any change at seven years which is different from expectation represents value added (or taken away) by the school. Such results might indeed be due to school factors, but they might also be due to a variety of other influences, within the child and/or the environment.

This model is useful in our examination of approaches to screening for SEN, to which we turn next, and to the measurement of value-added, discussed in Chapter 4.

Chapter 3

Screening for children with special educational needs

The identification of difficulties should be done earlier rather than later. This truism is at the heart of screening initiatives, whether in the medical or the educational domain. In this chapter we shall examine the various factors which need to be considered when developing and implementing a screening procedure, and in evaluating its effectiveness. We shall explore the extent to which a system applied to children on school entry at the age of about five years can identify children's difficulties and special educational needs.

In Chapter 1 we set out eight purposes for baseline assessment, one of which was the early identification of SEN. In this chapter we shall examine this purpose specifically. In this regard, the purpose of baseline assessment is to identify *children* and start to identify *specific developmental difficulties*. Note the two separate foci: the former is a process of identification, the latter one of assessment.

A model

When thinking about screening the tendency is to concentrate on an optimal model. In this there is a problem or disorder which is to be identified. This could be either a positive or negative attribute. For example, the current screening procedures adopted by secondary schools, often not explicitly, are designed to identify children with positive attributes. In the case of the 11 plus, the system was designed to identify the most able intellectually (the percentage varied from one LEA to another). In the case of secondary schools currently, many operate systems which take account of intellectual ability, religious affiliation and commitment, family commitment to education and other factors. Hence, the basic process here is one of *selection*. In the present discussion we shall focus on identification of children with difficulties but the basic issues generally pertain to other groups.

The first issue therefore, is to define the problem to be identified. In the optimal model this will be clear cut. Secondly, it must follow that the condition leads without exception to other developmental problems. In other words, it is *important*. Thirdly, these problems should have a direct solution, appropriate for all cases.

In practice, however, these absolutes and certainties tend not to exist, and the likelihood of relationships is measured in probabilities. But, even so, probabilities might be very high. For example, children with Down's syndrome were once thought ineducable, and assumed to be of similar abilities. Experience has shown that these children might have a range of abilities, albeit that a degree of intellectual impairment is present in all. An even better example is that of phenylketonuria (PKU). This metabolic disorder results in children not being able to process phenylalanine in food. As a result, intellectual impairment follows. There is now a simple and highly accurate screening procedure, the Guthrie test, which involves testing a small blood sample taken from a new born baby. Children with PKU are placed on special diets which greatly reduces the likelihood of intellectual impairment.

The question that arises is: to what extent can we assume that psychological and educational screening programmes at five years can be based on the same assumptions of high levels of certainty and prediction?

Evidence from health screening programmes

Before focusing on education, we shall first examine evidence on medical screening. Screening programmes for medical conditions have been regarded as inherently worthwhile, but in parallel with our criticism of baseline assessment (see Chapter 5) it is clear that evidence on medical screening has either been scanty or not encouraging. We have already used PKU as an example, and this is worth pursuing first. Early work showed clearly the impact of PKU on development and the benefits of modified diet (see Lindsay 1984 for a review). Subsequently it has been concluded that the value of screening programmes for PKU has been established (Hall 1996). They are expensive, but considered cost-effective. The test itself is effective, but care needs to be taken in its analysis in the laboratory, and to ensure good phenylalanine control in the first few years of life. Although its coverage is good, some children are missed (Streetly *et al*. 1994).

Other screening programmes are also possible at birth, e.g. for Duchenne muscular dystrophy and cystic fibrosis, but these are not carried out in all regions. The former is questioned in terms of cost-benefits, and the latter as there is no clear evidence of benefits arising from identification. While elevated levels of lead in blood and teeth are associated with intellectual impairment (Pocock *et al.* 1994), there is a lack of support for screening programmes in this country as the impact on cognitive functioning is considered small and there are doubts about the benefits of intervention and cost-effectiveness in children without other clinical evidence of lead intoxication (Hall 1996).

Screening for sensori-neural hearing impairment is considered to be important and necessary. This is the more serious type, involving damage to the cochlea or auditory nerve and is generally associated with higher degrees of hearing loss. Sensori-neural hearing loss (SNHL) without intervention has a high correlation with impaired language acquisition. The second type, conductive hearing loss, is associated with middle ear infections, secretory otitis media (SOM) or otitis media with effusion (OME). This has been found to be very common among children in early to middle childhood and especially among disadvantaged groups. Also, there is a high prevalence among children found to have specific and moderate learning difficulties. With respect to education, there is a link with the development of phonological awareness in children (see Haggard 1993 for a review), particularly in those children whose OME persists, or reappears frequently.

The screening of hearing impairment is not straightforward. There are methods which might be applied to babies. These have improved in reliability since these were reviewed in the early days (Lindsay 1984) but universal neonatal screening is still regarded as largely a research procedure (Hall 1996). What is recommended is selective screening of high risk children, and a review of the distraction test for babies, of about seven months, which are carried out in well baby clinics. These are simple, but research has suggested quality is often of an inadequate standard. In particular, inadequate testing might lead to the conclusion that the baby can hear, so undermining the parents' justified belief that there is a problem, and putting off necessary assessment and intervention.

In this brief review, we have highlighted some of the issues which have arisen in screening for medical conditions. Those conditions chosen all have educational implications, and a system of baseline assessment should connect with such medical programmes. But our second purpose is to indicate the problems involved in these different systems, including technical quality of the assessment, quality control of the analyses, access to the children, and unproven success of the intervention. This is not to argue that these procedures are not worthwhile; some are. But this review

33

does indicate the need to go beyond the simplistic assumption that early identification must be a good thing.

Factors to consider in a screening programme

Purpose

We shall focus on the identification of difficulties in this chapter, but the other two child-focused purposes specified in Chapter 1 are also relevant, identifying the stages of learning for all children, and providing starting points for teaching.

Having chosen this general area, there are still questions to ask. Do we wish to identify a general problem, specific problems, or a combination? For example, in the former we would probably require a method which covered a number of developmental factors including language, behaviour and social development. A specific programme might focus on hearing or on reading. For the benefit of teachers, a combination may be more helpful with results which provide a general picture, but also pointers to specific areas.

The Infant Index and Baseline-*plus*, for example, provide total scores indicating overall development, but also provide information on 15 specific aspects of development (e.g. speaking and listening, spelling, concentration) as well as group factors: basic skills and behaviour.

Identification and assessment

When deciding purpose it is important to separate identification and assessment. In our approach, identification is a coarser process which focuses on the child as a whole, and so is less specific. For example, screening programmes at this level might have the purpose of showing that a child has a problem with hearing, with vision, with spoken language, or reading. The judgement will be made against a particular scale. This may be *criterion-referenced*. In the case of hearing, for example, a child's acuity will be measured against standards – can he or she hear a sound of a particular frequency at minimum loudness. Or, as with reading, the cut-off might be *norm-referenced* using a reading age or standardised score.

Such processes lead to children being identified. For example, a screen of seven year olds might identify a group of children in a school with reading ages below the level expected at that age. This information must then be extended by an examination of the child's particular set of skills and knowledge relevant to the issue at hand. For example, a child with a 'reading problem' will be assessed to examine whether they know their letter sounds, can blend, are able to match letter sounds to written letters and so on.

One of the errors that can easily be made is to assume that a programme essentially designed for screening provides information which is more detailed than it really is. This is particularly so with instruments which produce several scores. If the procedure is designed as a screen, there will still be a need to have assessment.

A useful definition of screening, albeit taken from the medical field, is that of the American Commission on Chronic Illness in 1957:

> the presumptive identification of unrecognised disease or deficit by the application of tests, examinations and other procedures, which can be applied rapidly. Screening tests sort out apparently well persons who might have a disease from those who probably do not. A screening test is not intended to be diagnostic. (quoted in Hall 1996, p.83)

Screening for 'at risk' or present condition

Children who are screened at seven or nine years might be found to have a condition, for example that their reading or maths is at a specified low level. If we can identify these children likely to develop such problems before they occur, then we might be able to prevent these difficulties. In the latter case our focus is on children who are 'at risk' of developing problems, not those currently having the specified difficulties.

In practice, there is no simple relationship with age. A baseline assessment might help to identify children at risk of educational problems, but it might also usefully identify difficulties being experienced at that time. A child might, for example, be identified as having limited language at five years. This is important to act upon at that time for its own sake, not only as a preventative measure for later difficulties. Nevertheless, the identification of children 'at risk' is a key element in the purpose of baseline assessment.

The main issue for 'at risk' screening is the degree to which the aspects measured relate to the difficulties in which we are interested. Returning to our PKU analogy, the 'at risk' element is the presence of PKU while the condition to prevent is intellectual impairment. The two are linked biochemically and, importantly, the probability of the metabolic disorder leading to intellectual impairment is very high, close to certainty.

In the case of baseline assessment, therefore, we must assess the degree to which the factors measured at that time will lead to the later problems (e.g. poor reading at seven years), assuming no remediation is provided. In this case, rather than a special diet the remediation will be a form of educational input, e.g. extra or different teaching. Unfortunately, when it comes to psycho-educational factors, the degrees of relationship with later problems are much lower. No longer can we be certain that poor performance at five years will lead with a very high probability, approaching certainty, to educational problems at seven years. Indeed, research has indicated that the correlations between screening tests at five years and outcome measures at seven years might be only in the range 0.3 to 0.7. Even in the case of the highest correlations of about 0.7, only about half the variance is accounted for. In other words, even though the screening measure might be very significantly correlated with the seven year old measure, it will lead to a number of errors: children who pass the screen but later are considered to have educational difficulties – false negatives; and children who fail the screen but later do have difficulties – false positives (see below).

Hits and misses

In any screening procedure which is not perfect, there will two kinds of error:

false positives – children identified as 'failing' the baseline assessment at five years, but considered to be progressing satisfactorily at a later stage, say end of Key Stage 1

false negatives – children identified as 'passing' the baseline assessment but judged to have educational difficulties at end of Key Stage 1.

These outcomes, termed 'Misses', and the desirable outcomes, termed 'Hits', are represented in Figure 3.1. In the present discussion we are focusing on predicting children's status at the end of Key Stage 1 for baseline assessment, but this model of a screening instrument's accuracy applies also when the criterion is concurrent. For example, in the PKU analogy the screen is the blood test and the criterion is the presence of PKU. In this instance the hits and misses represent the concurrent accuracy of the test.

36

Results on screening test	Outcome at 7 years	
pass	true negative (HIT)	false negative (MISS)
fail	false positive (MISS)	true positive (HIT)
	pass	fail

Figure 3.1 Representation of 'hits' and 'misses' for screening test

Figure 3.1 suggests that the cells might be of comparable size. In practice this is usually not the case. For example, if we are screening five years olds to identify current or future difficulties we are more likely to want to identify a smaller number than the 50 per cent implied in Figure 3.1. A figure of about 15 per cent, possibly 20 per cent is commonly used. The 15 represents minus one standard deviation on many tests and the approximate range of children considered to have SEN at any particular time (about 1 in 6) or during their school lives (about 1 in 5). However, while these estimates derive from sound epidemiological studies (e.g. Rutter *et al.* 1970) and have been replicated in later studies which seek teachers' opinions (e.g. Croll and Moses 1985), they are, ultimately, derived from judgements, not hard data on 'real' problems.

If we take a cut-off of 15 per cent for each of the screening and the criterion measures, we can see the percentages that *should* occur in each cell (see Figure 3.2):

- of the children passing the screen, 100 per cent should pass the seven years measure (Cell A)
- similarly all those failing the screen should fail at seven years (Cell D)
- consequently the expected frequencies in both Cells B and C should be 0 per cent.

If we screen 1,000 children, then on these expectations Cell A should contain 850, and Cell D 150.

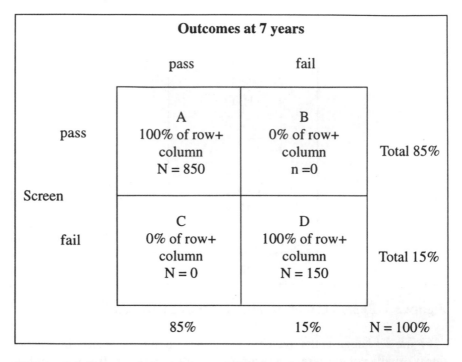

Figure 3.2 Expected percentage of 'hits' and 'misses' for cut-off at 15 per cent

If the screening test is not completely accurate and misclassified, say, 50 children, then Cell B would have 50, and Cell A would reduce to 800. This is not a huge drop in the percentage which are misclassified by the screening test. However, a figure of 50 in Cell C, i.e. children who failed the test but passed the seven year assessment, represents a high percentage of the accuracy of the 'fail' judgement of the screen, 50 out of 150 are 'misses'.

The same kind of analyses might be undertaken retrospectively by the percentage of children passing or failing the seven year old measure. The main point for the present discussion is that, given less than perfect predictions, a change of a given *number* of children might have disproportionate effects on the false positive against the false negative rates.

The implications for baseline assessment are:

- that the instrument should be as accurate as possible
- a decision must be made during its construction to optimise the relative number of false positives and false negatives.

The latter can be achieved by altering the cut-off. In the present case we chose 15 per cent, but this could be amended according to the priority with respect to the types of error. However, it is important to keep in mind that this must be done on an *educational* basis, not simply to make the best fit to a model. In our case, what is more important: to reduce the number of children incorrectly identified as being 'at risk' who later turn out to be within normal limits, or those incorrectly judged to be not 'at risk' who later fail? In the first case, children might be given inappropriate 'special' help which might cause problems, reduce other opportunities and waste resources. In the latter, children will miss out on necessary intervention.

It should also be noted that in this model we have not considered the accuracy of the seven year old measure, but taken this as perfect. In reality, or course, it is not. The National Curriculum assessments, for example, are open to criticism, e.g. Tymms (1997a) who is critical of the lack of precision in Key Stage 1 tests results and argues that

> There is a long way to go before the KSI data can be regarded as being of high quality. (p.7)

This does not reduce the importance of this evaluation of the screening measure, but does, in practice, make this more problematic.

Criteria for baseline assessment as screening procedures

We have outlined a number of factors which should be considered when developing and evaluating a baseline assessment procedure. The following is a summary of key factors taken from earlier guidance on screening by Wilson and Junguer (1968), and Cochrane and Holland (1969). Remember, baseline assessment is presented here as a form of screening, *not* detailed assessment.

Importance

The main aspect of interest must be importance. Language development, concentration, mathematics and social behaviour, for example, would be considered important at age five.

Simplicity

The procedure should be easy to operate. This implies minimal instructions, a small number of procedures and limited time. Implicit in this is that minimal training should be required, consequently scoring criteria must be clear, unambiguous and straightforward. Also implicit is that baseline assessment might be carried out by teachers, not more specialist practitioners including SEN support teachers, educational psychologists.

Acceptability

Parents, teachers and children should accept the need for this initiative, and the procedure in question. This appears to be the case in principle with respect to baseline assessment. For example, the SCAA consultation (SCAA 1997c) indicated a high level of support. In addition, the specific instrument/procedure must be acceptable. Teachers will be in the front line here and have a key view. Again, the SCAA consulted, and teachers expressed views about the three approaches piloted by SCAA (1996c, 1996d, Caspall *et al.* 1997).

Some schemes for early identification, however, have had elements which have caused questions or concern. For example, the Dyslexia Early Screening Test (Nicholson and Fawcett 1996) includes a balance item which requires the teacher to push the child (gently) to unbalance them. The inclusion of this test arose from research carried out by the authors which suggested this test could be useful, and justified on the basis of a model of information processing which they were developing, but teachers have complained to us that this in inappropriate.

Accuracy

Baseline assessment should provide an accurate judgement. Teachers and parents want to be sure that misclassifications do not occur. Unfortunately, as we have argued above, total accuracy is not possible. The most that can be requested is that the procedure has evidence for its accuracy, and that this accuracy is judged to be acceptable.

Sensitivity

As one element of accuracy, the procedure should maximise the number of identifications of children who have difficulties (true positives).

Specificity

Equally, the procedure should give a negative finding when the child does not have difficulties. As stated above, neither specificity nor sensitivity will be perfect; it is the level of each which must be judged.

Replicability

The procedure should provide comparable results independent of who carried it out and which day this happened within a short time-span (e.g. two weeks).

Links with intervention

There is little point identifying children if no specific action is to be taken. There must be direct links with specified interventions, which might be of different kinds if the baseline assessment produces profiles rather than a single score.

Links with assessment

Before moving on to intervention, teachers will need to consider further assessment. This need not be a separate stage, but could be built into an assessment–teaching–assessment cycle. Indeed, as baseline assessment will be limited to Stage 1 of the Code of Practice (see Chapter 7) the teacher will be the person to carry out the first stage of assessment.

Lack of ambiguity

The developmental factor under investigation should be clear and agreed. In medical screening this might be easily achieved, e.g. a specific metabolic disorder, or lack of function. Children at school entry, however, might be screened on one or more factors. What validity do these have? The Infant Index was developed on the basis of items proposed by experienced Reception teachers, so providing at least face validity. Other schemes have focused on early literacy, language and mathematics, which will also be non-controversial. Nevertheless, any baseline assessment scheme should be clear with respect to the target developmental aspect which is under consideration.

Improvement

Not only should there be a link with intervention, there should be evidence that this will be successful. The use of baseline assessment on all the nation's school entrants will lead to large numbers being identified as having, or at risk of developing, psycho-educational difficulties, e.g. in reading. As a result, schools might allocate these children to an educational experience which differs in some way from the norm. This might be by offering extra help of essentially the same kind; modified programmes, e.g. Reading Recovery; referrals (eventually) to other professionals, even eventually to special schools. All of this will be done with good intent, to help the child, but the question remains – will it work? Will these alternative educational experiences actually lead to improvement, and if so by how much?

If baseline assessment leads to such modifications, and the numbers involved are about 15 per cent, or 1 in 6, then over one million five year olds will be affected.

Cost-effectiveness

Baseline assessment, like all screening procedures, costs money and draws on other resources. The instruments themselves must be purchased, time for processing results must be paid for, and teacher time must be allocated. While the assessment is being carried out, teaching will be reduced or stopped either for that child, or larger numbers. This is acceptable, provided there are benefits and the procedure is cost-effective.

A developed model of baseline assessment

Earlier in this chapter we discussed a basic model. It is clear from subsequent discussion that this is insufficient. In Figure 3.3 we present a developed model which takes into account two different processes, reflecting the stage which most baseline assessment schemes have reached (see Chapter 5).

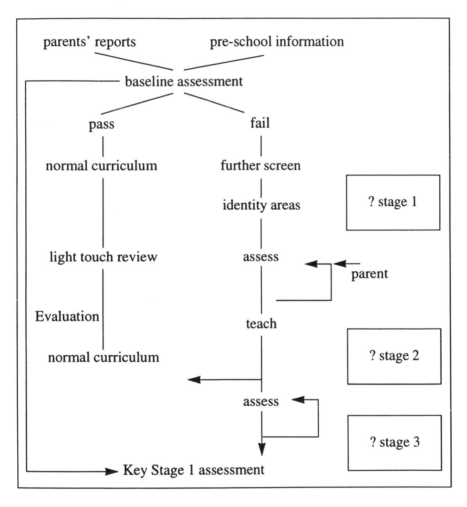

Figure 3.3 An elaborated model of a baseline assessment as a means of the early identification of special educational needs

The first of the two processes concerns the child.

- Before baseline assessment is carried out teachers should draw upon the information that might be available from parents and any pre-school provision.
- Baseline assessment should be carried out during the first half term in school.
- On the basis of this, a child might be designated as satisfactory, and continue to receive the normal curriculum (both content and teaching methods). Children identified as having difficulties should have their baseline assessment results examined in more detail. This requires, of course, that the procedure allows such detailed analyses. An example is provided in Chapter 6.
- There might then be a benefit in a further screening procedure. This might be carried out by the teacher, and at its simplest might be a repeat of the original baseline assessment. This has benefits where there might have been confounding factors, or the teacher might doubt his or her accuracy on the first trial. In other cases, a screening of hearing, for example, might be indicated, when language or attention are highlighted as problem areas.
- The next stage involves a more detailed assessment where this seems appropriate, linked with teaching. Hence, the teacher might conduct further exploratory work with the child to try to clarify areas of problems, or determine that the apparent problems are not, in fact, present. A profile indicating language problems, for example, might lead the teacher to work with the child on specific tasks designed to identify knowledge of basic vocabulary, use of sentence structure or more specific articulation difficulties. This assessment would be part of ongoing classwork, on the whole, and linked to teaching.
- At this point, the teacher would need to decide with the special educational needs coordinator (SENCO), whether the child should be registered at Stage 1 or 2 of the Code of Practice (see Chapter 7). Parents will have been kept involved, but will need to have a specific discussion at this point.
- Over the next period, which may be weeks or months, the teacher will modify parts of the curriculum, and assess the child's development. While this should be occurring to some degree for all children, those in this group will have a raised level of involvement from the teacher.
- While this is occurring, those children previously designated 'pass' will have had less frequent 'review'. By this we do not mean the

formal reviews of the Code of Practice, but that the teacher will occasionally, perhaps termly, undertake a specific, but 'light touch' assessment of how all these children are progressing. This will allow those who were misclassified as false negatives to be given the opportunity for a later identification.

- Over Key Stage 1, these twin tracks will continue. From time to time children should be 'moved' from one track to the other. That is, some children previously identified as having difficulties will be returned to the main group, and vice versa.
- At the end of Key Stage 1, the outcome measure will provide useful information on the two groups of children, allowing teachers to evaluate the effectiveness of their practice as well as recording the successes achieved by the children.

The second process concerns the evaluation of the baseline assessment procedure itself. As we argue in Chapter 5, at this time there is a dearth of technical information on many of the schemes. Normally, such a scheme would be of known validity and this second process might not be necessary. In this case, however, LEAs and schools would be advised to evaluate the success of their own scheme as an instrument in its own right. This will require an examination of its attributes against the criteria stated above. A more detailed set of examples is provided in Chapter 5.

Detection of difficulties or promotion of educational opportunities?

Within the medical domain, there has been a change in emphasis from detection and surveillance, to health promotion. This is exemplified in the most recent publication supported by the British Paediatric Association, the report of the Third Joint Working Party on Child Health Surveillance (Hall 1996). The first two editions had focused on child health surveillance and promoted the application of rigorous criteria for screening programmes. The new edition built upon this earlier work, with Sir Michael Peckham in the foreword arguing that the earlier guidance had had the desired effect. The emphasis now was on health promotion.

In this typology, there are three stages of prevention. Primary prevention applies to the reduction in incidence of cases of a disease or disorder. Secondary prevention is the focus of the present chapter, namely attempts to reduce the prevalence of a disease or disorder. Early identification is the mechanism whereby the impact might be reduced, as effective intervention might follow. Screening is one of the means for achieving this, others include parental referrals and other ad hoc identification instances.

Tertiary prevention is aimed at reducing the effects of impairments which cannot be prevented, including the adjustment of children and parents to the condition. Baseline assessment falls essentially into the secondary prevention category, as a form of screening. However, it is useful to consider this as part of a total system of the promotion of educational opportunities, to which we shall return in Chapter 9.

Conclusion

One of the purposes of baseline assessment is the early identification of SEN. Indeed, this was the main origin for the process, with many schools and LEAs having set up early identification procedures over the past 20 years or so. In this chapter we have examined the requirements of early identification schemes, and proposed a model of baseline assessment which links it into general planning at Key Stage 1, to the Code of Practice stages of identification and assessment.

There is now a variety of instruments available for children at school entry. Some have been developed specifically as baseline assessment for the purposes of value-added, for example the PIPs scheme (Tymms et al. 1997). Others were developed primarily as means for the early identification of difficulties and SEN. The Infant Rating Scale (Lindsay 1981) is an example of this approach. While some, including the Infant Rating Scale and Infant Index, attempt to cover a wide range of children's development, others are designed for more specific purposes.

One of the most recent is the Dyslexia Early Screening Test (Nicholson and Fawcett 1994). This, as its title implies, is designed to identify children who are likely to develop specific learning difficulties/dyslexia and is a reaction to the earlier tendency to put off both assessment and intervention until the child was about seven years old, when the discrepancy between their actual literacy development and that predicted on the basis of their general ability could be assessed.

The third group of instruments have been developed for one purpose, but might then be used for another. For example, the Infant Index was originally developed as a means of identifying children with SEN but schools then wished to use it to assess value-added, and the LEA considered it useful as an educational measure to determine the SEN element in the schools budget formula for infant schools, and schools with infant departments.

As described in Chapter 6, the Infant Index has now been developed as a baseline assessment scheme for use as part of the government's statutory requirements of schools. As such it has been further developed, as a computer-marked system entitled Baseline-*plus*.

We have argued that a simple model is inadequate, as an approach to the early identification of children with SEN. Rather, baseline assessment might provide a useful, and indeed key element in the process of early identification and secondary prevention of SEN. The important concept here is *process*. The instruments and the procedure as a whole should meet the criteria set out earlier in this chapter, or at least show high degrees of concordance. But the point about pycho-educational difficulties is that it is not possible to assume a one to one correspondence between the indicators produced by the screening instrument and the basic condition, and there is a similar lack of high certainty between difficulties identified and interventions necessary for success. As a consequence, what is required is a process, over time, using high quality instruments, but integrated into a continuous system of monitoring children's development.

Chapter 4

Value-added

Evaluating schools, and making judgements about their performance, is deceptively simple. We take a few performance indicators, measure these accurately and then compare the results of one school with another, or with local schools, or against the national picture. In this way we, as parents, pupils or members of the general public, will be able to judge which are good schools, which are poor, or average. The question arises, however: is life so simple? In fact, the answer is clearly that it is not. Such simple, some might argue simplistic, evaluations might produce results which are positively misleading. In a period where such information is readily available, indeed actively promoted, such mis-information may be highly damaging to the school whose performance is underestimated. Equally, the presentation of data which overestimates a school's performance may result in parents and pupils, both those already associated with the school or potential applicants, being misled.

In this chapter we shall explore the attempts to address these problems and develop instead an evaluation and assessment system which is more robust and useful than the simple model alluded to above. The main aspect we shall examine is that which has come to be called 'value-added'. This refers to the difference a school has made beyond that which might be expected. Our focus is on the use of baseline assessment as a contribution to value-added measures, but we shall place this specific discussion within the wider context of value-added developments in schools.

The origins of value-added

We shall focus on two main contributions to the development of value-added measures, namely the general drive for 'quality', and the specific initiatives designed to 'correct' simple evaluations of schools which do not take account of factors considered relevant to a valid analysis of their performance.

The search for quality

A criticism of many organisations within the public sector was that they were failing to provide a sense of the appropriate quality, and that they failed to give value for money. This analysis is particularly associated with the period starting with the Thatcher government. However, in education it can be traced back as a significant issue to the Ruskin College speech made by Jim Callaghan in 1976 when Prime Minister. He raised concerns, as a non-educationist, about the standard of education. His speech raised important questions about the curriculum and the *control* of the curriculum, the 'secret garden'.

Of course, there has always been some concern about the education service (along with the National Health Service and other public institutions). The difference was one of scale. In general, public concerns had been focused on limited parts of the system, for example, the William Tyndale school in Islington during the mid 1970s. There had also been more wide-ranging concerns expressed by the academic community, together with some practitioners and politicians. The Black Papers, for example, which began publication in the late 1960s, provided trenchant criticism of the education service (e.g. Cox and Dyson 1971). But here we had the Prime Minister starting a 'great debate'.

The concern for quality was also reflected in the worlds of business and commerce. Many companies began to examine their own performance, and a series of seminal texts were produced by management consultants. One of the most significant was *In Search of Excellence* by Peters and Waterhouse (1982) reporting case studies of major US companies, all of which had been highly successful. On the basis of these analyses, the authors proposed principles to guide managers of other companies in achieving similar success.

At the same time, a number of management systems were developed which addressed the issue of quality. One which became particularly common was Total Quality Management (TQM). This was based upon the premise that a product should be *fit for the purpose*. It originated with the US military for its suppliers and was picked up by industries beyond those. TQM also found favour in non-industrial and service organisations, including public services, who sought to achieve the standard of performance which matched the requirements of British Standard 5750.

Hence, within the education service, including schools, LEA administrations and support services there was a developing concern for 'quality'. While some saw this as a necessary component of professionalism and hence a matter of proper and positive endeavour, for many the pace was forced by the increasing marketisation of education and other public services. In particular, the 1988 Education Reform Act required LEAs to delegate finance to schools, and for schools to take responsibility for their own management. Information about schools (and LEAs) would be more visible through National Curriculum assessments, and the reports following inspection by OFSTED, and the governors' report to the parents of schools at an annual meeting.

With the exception of the annual meeting of parents for governors to report, which is commonly poorly attended, and in some cases have had no parent other than governors present, the public and media have shown interest in the information provided by these initiatives. Consequently, the desire of schools and other institutions to have the optimal organisation and levels of achievement has been given added impetus. Methods vary, with many preferring a quality assurance approach, which attempts to ensure the system is functioning properly in the first place, rather than focus on inspection of the outcomes. The aim should be services which are fit for the purpose rather than aiming for perfection (Lindsay 1996).

The problems of 'raw' data

While schools might prefer to focus on quality assurance, the politicians had set up assessment and reporting systems which required, in different forms, a quality control approach. Schools had to report the results of the National Curriculum assessments, GCSE and A level. In addition, rates of exclusion and attendance were added to the information which had to be released into the public domain. At least in the early stages, the media have showed much interest. For example, in 1997 national newspapers devoted space to reporting the National Curriculum test results. The broadsheets, in particular, typically produced supplements of many pages. For example, the *Guardian* published a 20 page supplement listing all secondary schools' GCSE results (20 November) and a 13 page report of all primary schools' Key Stage 2 results (11 March).

However, these results were raw data. That is, they reported the results of the pupils for each school but did not take into account the advantages some schools might have which were not of their own making. For example, take four children whose results on a reading test are presented in Table 4.1 at two points, when they are seven and again when nine years old.

Table 4.1 Improvement in reading age for four girls

	Reading age		
	7 years	9 years	Gain
Stacie	7.0	9.0	2
Nicki	8.0	10.0	2
Melissa	6.0	9.0	3
Chloe	9.0	10.0	1

Stacie had a reading age of 7 and then 9 and so could be said to be attaining at her age level on each occasion. Nicki however had a reading age of 8 initially, and then 10 when retested when she was nine years old. She might be described as a year ahead of her chronological age in reading on each occasion. Now consider the third child, Melissa. She had a reading age of 6 initially, a year behind, but scored at her age level when nine years old. Lastly, Chloe scored at 9 years originally, two years ahead, and at 10 years on the second occasion.

These results show four girls, each with a different profile. But there are two ways of evaluating these results. Firstly, we might look at *absolute* levels of attainment. In this case, only Stacie was at her age level when seven years old. Nicki and Chloe were advanced by one and two years respectively, while Melissa was a year behind her chronological age level. If we now consider the results when the girls were nine years old we find that Stacie and Melissa are at their age level, while Nicki and Chloe are a year advanced.

Secondly, consider the *rate* of improvement in attainment. While two girls improved two years in their reading age over two years of schooling, Melissa improved by *three* years over this period. Also, one of the girls with the highest reading age at nine years, Chloe, improved by only 1 year. These four girls reveal the importance of measuring not only *absolute levels* of attainment, but also *rate of progress*.

Now, substitute a school for each girl, and the mean (average) level of attainment in each case. The situation is parallel. We can see in Table 4.2 that two schools, B and D, have the highest mean reading ages when pupils are nine years old, but one of these (school D) reported an improvement of only 1 year over two years, while school C, although only achieving average attainment, reported the highest mean gain of 3 years.

How should a school's results be reported? There is nothing improper in the present system insofar as absolute levels of attainment are reported (leaving aside the questions of the technical quality of the tests, to which we shall return). But only reporting these will seriously misrepresent the situation. School D's inferior progress, and school C's superior progress will go unnoticed.

Table 4.2 Improvement in mean reading age for four schools

	Mean reading age		
	7 years	9 years	Gain
School A	7.0	9.0	2
School B	8.0	10.0	2
School C	6.0	9.0	3
School D	9.0	10.0	1

The purpose of value-added

So far we have focused on the use of assessments for purposes of accountability, to meet reporting requirements. There is a second important purpose which reflects the other reason schools and others became interested in quality initiatives. This is the desire for schools to have optimal systems, and hence produce the best results to match their aspirations. Given that schools have usually taken the view that their systems and results could be better, this process has become known as 'school improvement'. In this case, however, the purpose of collecting the information is to inform the institution itself, the teachers and governors in particular, to support formulation of plans to improve performance. Hence, the same approach, at least in principle, could be used for each purpose. However, as we shall come on to see, there are important issues to consider when a school's data are being reviewed for one purpose or the other.

Accountability

The thrust towards increased accountability is clear. The government now publishes 'league tables', as they were once known, or 'performance tables' as the present government now describes them. In these, school results are presented to the public who are able to make comparisons. For example, tables for GCSE and A level were published in the *Guardian* (18 November 1997), and other newspapers. Each LEA's results are presented and it can be seen that for example in Coventry 11 per cent of pupils achieved five or more GCSE grades A–C in one school, while in a second 99 per cent achieved this level. This information allows the public therefore to compare one school with another. In this sense the results improve accountability.

In terms of purpose, what does accountability achieve? There is a clear belief amongst members of the present Labour government, as in the previous Conservative government, that such accountability will help to drive up standards. The publication of results will energise schools to do better. We have chosen to call this *accountability* as it results in each school being held to account. But there are at least two client groups amongst parents: those of children in the school and those of potential applicants. The former want to see the school serving their child; the latter need to decide whether this is the appropriate school for their child.

School effectiveness

School effectiveness has a different, academic and professional tradition. Research was carried out aimed at attempting to identify which schools were effective, and how this occurred. In these studies schools are exemplars and so are *anonymous* in the research report. The aim is to identify key factors which can be examined in other schools to determine generalisability. Good examples of this approach include *Fifteen Thousand Hours* (Rutter *et al.* 1979) for secondary schools, and *School Matters: The Junior Years* (Mortimore *et al.* 1988).

Also in this tradition are comparisons of different types of school, particularly selective versus comprehensive, and single sex versus mixed intakes. A number of studies have examined differential effects *within* schools with respect to progress of children of different ethnic background, or the different subject departments in secondary schools.

School Improvement

The third purpose is effectively where the first two come together. The evidence from school effectiveness studies has been combined with the wish to go beyond the desire to drive up standards simply on the basis of publicity. There are different approaches. These include 'blame and shame' where the 'worst schools' are publicly castigated; the engagement of advisers/consultants to aid improvement; and the school's own internal action to improve its standards. One point to note is that the school improvement process may be private, concerning only those intimately involved with the school (teachers, governors, possibly parents and pupils), or nationally recognised in a blaze of publicity. For example, the latest performance tables were accompanied with a list of the 'hundred fastest improving schools in England' as measured by increases in rates of pupils achieving five or more GCSE at grades A–C. The 'top' school, the greatest improver, recorded a change from 27 per cent to 64 per cent over the period 1994–97.

On the other hand the School Curriculum and Assessment Authority (1997a) asserts:

> All the evidence indicates that, given the right balance of pressure and support, standards rise fastest where schools themselves take responsibility for their own improvement. Many of the most effective schools succeed in raising pupils' attainment, sometimes quite dramatically, by setting standards for improvement based on how the pupils are currently performing and taking specific action to meet those targets. (p.1)

Value-added

Concern with raw data did not prevent the previous government publishing the results of national assessments on all schools, and this practice has continued into the first year of the new government. However, both sets of politicians as well as government departments have recognised the difficulties with the raw data used up to now. For example, to return to the Coventry data, the current tables do provide more information. School A with 11 per cent grades A–C at GCSE is a mixed comprehensive with 703 pupils, 38 per cent of whom are designated as having special educational needs. School B, on the other hand, while similar in size with 867 pupils, is a selective independent mixed school with no children specified as having SEN.

What should a value-added approach include?

In order to evaluate schools' effectiveness and hence any improvement they might make, it is necessary to be able to judge more than the simple output data. One common factor to build into the equation, therefore, is the educational achievements of pupils on entry to the school. Comparison at the end of the stage (e.g. the end of Key Stage 4) may now be by *differential progress* as well as attainment, as was shown in Table 4.2 . The government intends to introduce such analyses in the near future, possibly 1999.

But what should be the extra factors to feed into the analyses? Prior attainment may be supplemented by an estimate of social disadvantage, probably in the form of percentage of children receiving free school meals. This is a generally robust and valid measure of disadvantage (but see below) and would have an important effect on the performance tables.

But what of other factors? For example, we might include background characteristics (e.g. gender, ethnicity) or other influences on attainment over the time within the school in addition to attainment on entry. On the other hand we might not limit our analyses to educational outcomes, important though these are. We could measure the school's success in keeping its pupils (i.e. low exclusions, low transfer to other schools), or social outcomes (low rates of delinquency, high rates of pro-social behaviour).

There is, then, a question of the *measures* that might be used to assess value-added. These will reflect the importance that is attributed to different aspects of the educational performance of schools, or possibly just the measures that are easiest to obtain. For example, it is easier to analyse value-added for junior and secondary schools using end of key stage assessments because the data are available and the data can be analysed simply and quickly using statistical packages. Hence the junior stage may be examined by comparing the end of Key Stage 1 results at seven years with end of Key Stage 2 results at 11 years. But we need to recognise that this biases the evaluation of schools. Despite its failings, the OFSTED system of school inspection does allow, indeed requires, a comprehensive examination of the school's contribution, not only academic but also in terms of pupil behaviour, and moral and spiritual welfare, for example. But many of these are less easy to assess.

Fitz-Gibbon (1995) reports that the Advisory Group to the project investigating value-added recommended that any system should meet four criteria. It should be:

- readily understandable
- statistically valid
- not an undue burden on schools
- cost-effective.

The Advisory Group also argued that a value-added system should provide information that is 'useful for public accountability and for internal school improvement effort' (p.2).

Several studies have investigated the technical and practical aspect of the use of value-added measures. Jesson (1996) examined 12 schools, using Key Stage 3 data as a prediction of GCSE. The Fitz-Gibbon study comprises separate initiatives on primary schools, using Key Stage 1 results to predict Key Stage 2, and in secondary schools, using Key Stage 3 results to predict GCSE. (See also Tymms and Henderson 1995, Trower and Vincent 1995). In addition, Tymms (1996) has examined the use of baseline assessment for value-added. This work will be examined in more detail in Chapter 5, but for the present will be used to supplement information on the four criteria specified above.

Readily understandable

The basic concept of value-added is very simple – what does a school add to a child's progress over and above that which might reasonably be expected given certain factors? However, as we saw in the previous section, the determination of these factors, and indeed of the outcome measure(s), is not unproblematic. Here we shall focus on technical matters.

Value-added systems rely on statistical analyses. These may be of two variables, e.g. a baseline assessment score to measure overall Key Stage 1 assessment results, or a Key Stage 3 points score to predict GCSE total points score. Alternatively, a richer analysis may examine the relative relationships between, say, a simple predictor (e.g. total baseline assessment score) and a number of outcomes measures (e.g. each Key Stage 1 National Curriculum assessment individually). Finally, there may be comparisons of several predictors against several outcome measures. For example, the Baseline-*plus* (Desforges and Lindsay with Edexcel 1998) provides not only a total score but also two composite scores (see Chapter 6). Each of these might be compared with different Key Stage 1 subject outcomes. Hence it is necessary to determine how much complexity is helpful.

But this depends on purpose. For a national scheme, simplicity is required, otherwise performance tables might become unwieldy. Typically the current secondary tables provide only two GCSE scores: percentage of children scoring five or more Grade A*–C, and percentage obtaining at least one GCSE Grade A*–G. It is likely that the national baseline assessment schemes will publish, and hence require, a single baseline assessment score, and this will be compared with a single Key Stage 1 score. But a school, for its own purposes of improving its knowledge and determining a basis for action, would probably prefer a richer data set. Teachers might welcome the opportunity to compare educational and learning characteristics at school entry, and behavioural characteristics at this time *separately* with end of Key Stage 1 results.

A second issue concerns the nature of the statistical analyses and the degree to which the process is understood by key players – certainly teachers and parents, but also pupils. The statistical techniques available are complex and not immediately understandable, but some are more accessible than others. Research continues on the issue, but Fitz-Gibbon (1995, 1997) argues that the simple and understandable procedures give results which did not differ in practical terms from the results derived from more complex analyses.

Statistical validity

It is a basic requirement for test producers that they investigate the validity and reliability of their instruments. For example, the manuals of the Infant Index and Baseline-*plus* provide information on both of these. It would be expected that any new reading test or test of general cognitive ability would not be published unless such information were provided. The purpose is, initially, quality assurance. Proper investigation of these issues should ensure that published instruments are of appropriate quality. Furthermore, publication of this information allows users to decide whether the instrument will meet their needs, and enables researchers to appraise the technique critically.

Measurement of value-added is no different, in principle. However as *change* is being investigated, the requirement for demonstrable validity and reliability applies to *both* measures: the predictor and the outcome. The studies discussed above have begun to provide such information, and some baseline assessment instruments allow this to be done. But, as we shall argue below, this is far from universal. The recommendation by Fitz-Gibbon that simple statistical techniques are as appropriate as more complex techniques is encouraging, but this still requires that individual schemes have robust measures. It is of interest to note that the current SCAA/QCA criteria (SCAA 1997d) do not require *any* evidence of the technical quality of baseline assessment measures, let alone define a minimal standard (see Accreditation Criteria, Chapter 1, Figure 1.2).

There are four requirements for the schemes themselves. These address coverage, planning, nature of the outcome (a numerical score), and timing of administration. The further criteria address practical aspects of implementation. There is no reference to the technical quality of the scheme. Consequently it is possible that a scheme might meet all of these criteria and be manageable, cover the appropriate range of children's development, and be clear when the scheme should be administered. It might produce a numerical score for each child and provide information that allows teachers to plan. But the basic information collected might be unreliable, invalid and misleading. Children developing well, for example, might appear as children 'at risk' and vice versa. The accreditation criteria do not ensure that a minimum, let alone optimal level of technical quality is met.

Given that such schemes will be used to enable schools to be judged one against another, or against national trends, this is a sorry state of affairs. Remember also that the evidence of recent ministerial action is to 'name and shame'. Will it be the case that in four years' time schools will be named and shamed for their poor value-added on the basis of instruments of unknown, possibly inferior quality? In Chapter 5 we examine the technical quality of some of the scales available.

There is also another complication. Value-added analyses require both the baseline assessment and the outcome measure to be of acceptable reliability and validity. Consequently we must ask questions also of the quality of the end of Key Stage 1 assessments. The outcome measures in the secondary phase, GCSE grades, have shortcomings but these are well established and have been subject to research over many years. End of Key Stage 1 assessments, however, are not of such known worth. Indeed, early assessments were found to be far from satisfactory. For example, consider the results we obtained in comparing Key Stage 1 Reading scores with the Individual Reading Analysis (Vincent and de la Mare 1990) given shortly after. As can be seen from Table 4.3, the Key Stage 1 scores, while correlating with the Individual Reading Analysis scores to some extent, were very poor discriminators in the middle range. In fact, children recorded at Level 2 had reading ages from below 5.0 to over 10 years! A similar result was found for the Comprehension score, and when comparisons were made between SATs and the Word Reading Test of the British Ability Scales (Daniel 1996, Daly 1997).

Consider also the results of two schools' Key Stage 2 results as presented in Table 4.4. Are these fluctuations true reflections of pupil performance, teacher performance, or test validity?

Table 4.3 Key Stage 1 Reading assessments (range of Individual Reading Analysis Reading scores at each SAT level)

	IRA reading	Accuracy	Score
SAT level	Mean	SD	Reading age range
W	0	0	below 5.0 years
1	3.9	4.64	below 5–5.8 years
2	26.1	13.61	below 5–10.2 years
3	44.4	3.71	8.9–10.3 years

Table 4.4 Variation in two schools' Key Stage 2 results over three years

		% at Level 4 or greater		
		1995	1996	1997
English	school A	67	76	92
	school B	48	28	41
Maths	school A	90	76	88
	school B	39	20	45
Science	school A	93	79	92
	school B	80	25	56

Manageability

Schools have been under increasing pressure over the last ten years. They now must manage their budgets, and their own affairs to a larger degree; the support of LEAs has been diminished by the 1988 Education Reform Act; and subsequent legislation has had its effects. In addition, the National Curriculum, OFSTED inspections and the increase in publicity and accountability all take time as well and increase pressure. All schools are essentially in a market, and must attract pupils. This is more so for secondary schools where more parents tend to consider schools other than that which is local. Consequently, the additional action required to undertake a value-added analysis must be carefully considered with respect to workload and pressure. On the other hand, the greater

59

availability of information technology, and of packages which allow ready analyses, provide schools with more information at their fingertips.

The secondary value-added systems discussed here are all relatively easily manageable, using results for assessments which have been undertaken anyway. Some researchers have offered a service to schools and LEAs to process these data and provide information on value-added, but for their own purposes as well. Even extending the range of input and output measures will not greatly increase the time necessary for analyses, although more data might of course lead to much greater deliberation, trying to make sense of this wider range of information.

At primary and school entry, however, manageability is more of an issue. It should be remembered that these schemes all involve some extra work for teachers, typically at least 20 minutes per child. However, the SCAA/QCA criteria do specify that schemes must be manageable, and also the scheme providers must receive approval for their arrangements for data processing. The evidence from our own work (Desforges and Lindsay 1996) and of the NFER evaluation of the SCAA scheme (Caspell *et al.* 1997) suggests that these schemes are found to be manageable by teachers. Evidence on other schemes is not always available.

Cost-effectiveness

This is a more difficult criterion to evaluate schemes against. What would effectiveness be, let alone cost-effectiveness? The costs of a scheme are mainly in teacher time, data processing and analyses. The former is of little consequence in secondary schools, as the tests are already in place. Data analysis costs could vary. But the picture at school entry might be more problematic given the lack of a pre-existing system from which to use data, or an agreed single scheme. We can evaluate cost-effectiveness of different schemes, comparing one with another. But the larger question, which is true of *all* ages, is less easy to answer, although more important. What will be gained from these analyses at all, and how can this be measured against costs? It might well be that value-added schemes, properly devised and implemented, will be fairer.

Baseline assessment schemes tend to involve teachers in active examination of their pupils, unlike those at later stages where test data might simply be analysed. Typically, baseline assessments comprise either teacher ratings of the pupils' learning and behaviour or individually administered tasks, whether 'pencil and paper' or using a computer, or a mixture, and should be limited to a time allocation of about 20 minutes per pupil. But will this be *cost-effective* compared with having done nothing. For the purpose of internal school improvement, a staff and governors might well find this process is money well spent. Information might show where action needs to be taken to improve quality. For the purposes of national performance tables, it is worth re-emphasising that the need for value-added analysis is because of the inherent limitations in the use of raw data.

Other problematic features

In addition to the technical quality of the instrument *per se*, a value-added system must also be workable, and not only in the sense to be discussed in the next section. Information from the studies sponsored by SCAA for the design of national value-added schemes suggests this is problematic (Fitz-Gibbon 1997).

Pupil mobility

Value-added measures rely on the same children being measured on both occasions, otherwise change cannot be measured. But children move from one school to another, and for different reasons. For some this is part of a general trend, for example when parents change jobs or take up a job elsewhere, but for others the reason might be concerned with dissatisfaction with the school.

We are aware from our own work in areas of acute disadvantage of children rotating around a small number of schools as parents or pupils fall out with one after another or with the school. This is likely to be a minor problem, but pupil mobility in general is not. For example, Tymms and Henderson (1995) reports that only 53 per cent of pupils among a sample of 3,548 did *not* change schools before the end of Key Stage 2. Tymms argues that cohorts of about 30 pupils would be needed to allow reliable assessments at Year 6, and hence the school's intake would need to be about 60 in order to allow for about half the children moving. However, Fitz-Gibbon also reports that the DfEE database suggests only 15 per cent of primary schools had cohorts of over 60 children. Furthermore, pupil turnover is not uniform across cohorts.

With respect to baseline assessment, it might be that pupil turnover is less during Key Stage 1, but it is still likely to be significant, and to differ between schools. What is to be done? It is possible to construct rules, for

61

example by tracking children from one school to another and counting only those children who have spent a designated period in the school where the output is assessed. How long should this be? Or alternatively these children could be ignored in the analysis, but suppose they are an atypical group? In this case we lose valuable information – especially true if the purpose is internal school improvement, when examination of the scores for such subgroups might be very important.

Once again we have an example of a conflict of purpose. For the purpose of accountability and fairness, we might remove these data: for internal school improvement we should keep then in.

Size of school and pupil absence

In addition to mobility, pupils may have long periods of absence which affect their attainment. These might be sustained, or a series of shorter periods. A high proportion of chronic non-attenders comprise children with serious social disadvantage, and where physical and mental health problems within the family are common. Should such children be included? This depends on whether the school is seen as ensuring good attendance, or such children lead to an unfair appraisal of the school.

A second issue concerns absence at the time of assessment. If grading of schools is important, will some children be 'omitted' from the analyses if their data are likely to lead to impact negatively on the status of the school?

In general, pupil absence is less of an issue at the primary stage, but differential 'chasing up' of children to ensure they and the school have the benefit of baseline assessment might well vary across schools. This is more of an issue when discrete testing is required rather than completion of rating scales over a short period of time.

Gender

The evidence from the Fitz-Gibbon and Jesson studies, for example, indicates that, starting from the same point at Key Stage 3, girls tend to achieve higher at GCSE than do boys – that is, on average, they make more progress. Evidence further indicates that girls score higher than boys at the school entry. Strand (1997) reports that the Wandsworth scheme identified substantial differences in pupil progress between schools over the period from school entry to end of Key Stage 1, with girls being superior.

Value-added and social disadvantage

In our earlier discussion of value-added we reported that the usual measure is the level of attainment of the pupils at the beginning of the period of schooling under consideration, e.g. using Key Stage 3 data to determine expected GCSE scores, or GCSE scores to predict A level scores. There is a sound reason for this. Research has consistently demonstrated that the best prediction of later performance is current level of performance (e.g. Fitz-Gibbon 1997).

An alternative approach takes account of social disadvantage. One of the most telling criticisms of raw score league tables is that they demonstrate that schools in affluent areas do better than those in the inner cities, and other areas of social disadvantage. A fairer approach, consequently, would be to take account, or partial out, the influence of social disadvantage and then compare those new scores. Does the same pattern remain, or will we find that schools in very disadvantaged areas are achieving levels of improvement which are equal to or greater than the rates achieved by their more affluent neighbours?

The *Observer* on 23 November 1997 presented an analysis by the National Foundation for Education Research of the 1997 GCSE data. In this re-analysis, the GCSE score was different from that in the government's tables, being an average point score (where grade A* = 8, A = 7, B = 6. etc.) rather than percentage of children gaining five grades A* to C, or A* to G. This in itself would lead to some variation, but is arguably fairer.

Of more interest here is the use of three other scores. For each school, the table presented: percentage of free schools meals, percentage of pupils with special educational needs and percentage of pupils with English as a second language. These four scores were then analysed to produce an 'Observer' score defined as 'the degree to which the school is outperforming others with a similar intake' (page II of supplement), although the formula for this analysis is not provided.

On the basis of this re-analysis, the *Observer* published 'Our top 100 state schools'. This table presents a very different picture compared with the national performance tables. For example Hackney, an LEA with the lowest percentage of schools where pupils gained at least five GCSEs at A* to C, had three schools in the top eleven. The school second on the *Observer* list, Clapton, recorded only 23 per cent of pupils with five GCSEs at A* to C, compared with the national average of 44.5 per cent.

In a separate analysis the *Observer* presented information on the 'Value added top 1000 schools'. This resulted from an analysis of GCSE results from 3,000 schools, but was limited to the use of the number of pupils taking free school meals in each school. This information is presented by LEA, rather than a single list from 'the best' overall. Interestingly, Clapton school now has a 'value-added' score of 22.14, which places it in the middle of the list of Hackney schools published – these range from 11.98 to 34.04.

These analyses demonstrate the difficulties inherent in this procedure. If we argue that raw scores are unfair, what do we modify these by in order to make them fair? Here we have two different approaches producing different results. Each can be justified in principle. Free school meals entitlement is a good indicator of social disadvantage (see Marsh 1997) and social disadvantage has been found to correlate well with impaired educational and other developmental factors. But it is not necessarily a good reflector of 'cultural' disadvantage. For example, in a recession the numbers of children entitled to free school meals will include those from more homes, in terms of common definitions of social class, regarded as advantaged. Senior managers, teachers, engineers, scientists, etc., may all lose their jobs. This may not make a large impact on national figures, but consider a school serving a small community which most local children attend. If the major employer closes down, the percentage of pupils on free schools meals could increase. As a result, the school's results would be enhanced by this factor. On the other hand, take a school in a working class area of high unemployment when a new employer opens up resulting in a large proportion of local families coming off benefits. That school's value-added results will be reduced as a result of this change in employment. Is this fair?

The first table described may therefore appear preferable, having a wider range of variables, so reducing the impact of any one. But consider the validity of the column 'percentage of children with special educational needs'. This is not an objectively defined number, but represents the school's view of the percentage. Schools vary in their methods of determining this percentage and LEAs also differ in their involvement and direction of this. Consequently while the use of social disadvantage and SEN indicators has an appeal, there are important conceptual and practical issues to be addressed.

Fitz-Gibbon (1997) argues that the most important factor to take as the predictor is prior attainment, which accounts for about half of the variation in GCSE and end of key stage testing. She argues that adding in extra factors, including social indicators, contributes little to the prediction of relative progress, *at the level of the individual pupil*. However, at the level of the school, such indicators could have an important effect. For example, over 60 per cent of pupils were eligible for free school meals in ten per cent of the schools in their sample. Their progress was less, by about 0.2 of a key stage level, than the average school with 20 per cent of pupils on free school meals.

The inclusion of such data presents a dilemma depending again on purpose. For internal school improvement it is likely to be helpful to have an understanding of the impact of such social disadvantage factors. It is, however, important that this is not used as an excuse – a line strongly taken in a general context in the White Paper *Excellence in Schools* (DfEE 1997a).

Improvement

A second analysis which was carried out in 1997 concerns change in the raw data of schools' GCSE results over the period 1994–7. These tables were produced by the DfEE along with 'Top Performances Highlighted in New Performance Tables – Blunkett'. The *Times Educational Supplement*, 21 November 1997, presented the '100 most improved schools' and offered 'Congratulations', while also naming the '100 schools showing the biggest decline' and offering 'Commiserations'.

This analysis of changes in the percentages of pupils achieving GCSE grades A* to C does provide a measure of improvement, irrespective of the measured characteristic of the intake. For example, the school rated top changed from 27 to 64 per cent of pupils achieving A* to G grades, while the school which was top of the 100 schools showing greatest decline saw its percentage drop from 67 to 43 per cent.

However, several points may be made of this type of analysis. First, inspection of the tables reveals that the improvers tended to have lower scores initially. The 1994 results of the top ten schools ranged from nought to 31 per cent. The 'top ten decliners' on the other hand showed 1994 results of between 27 and 67 per cent. In terms of average scores, the improvers had a mean of 18.7 per cent GCSE grades A* to C passes in 1994, while the decliners had a mean of 49.4 per cent.

In other words, the improvers started from a much lower base. On the other hand, examination of the 1997 results shows a mean of 48.7 and 28.3 per cent respectively, so the relative change of the schools is important. However, the initial starting point of the school is also a relevant factor – at the extreme, a school originally achieving 100 per cent success can only stand still or be a decliner.

Secondly, it is important to recognise the effects of minor changes in

65

raw scores which may have very large effects in such tables. For example, the tenth school in the improvers' list had an increase of 27 per cent, while the 'bottom' of this list had 21 per cent. In a school where 100 pupils take GCSE, getting six more to achieve this level could have had a dramatic effect in this school's placing. The same applies, of course, to the decliners but in reverse. Such changes will be much more important in the middle of the distribution of all the country's secondary schools, where a change of just one per cent is likely to alter positions by tens if not hundreds of places.

Thirdly, this effect will be exaggerated in schools with low numbers. Interestingly the hundredth improver school is reported to have only ten pupils, so the achievement of 20 per cent GCSEs in 1997 (from nought per cent in 1994) was based on the results of just two pupils! If the school had managed to help just two more pupils achieve this level they would have been the 'top school' with 40 per cent improvement.

Fourthly, these tables give no indication of possible causes. Did the nature of the entry change? Did teaching improve? With respect to internal school improvement evaluations this issue is unproblematic. The raw data can be compared with associated variables and possible causes can be identified and evaluated. Changes made on the basis of such analyses can be evaluated over subsequent years. This is very different from the public reporting of the school as these tables provide.

The same issues concern analyses of LEAs. These were also listed by the *Times Educational Supplement* on 21 November 1997, with Newham as 'top improver' at 10.4 per cent – a rise from 23 to 33.4 per cent of pupils achieving GCSE grades A* to C in 1994 and 1997 respectively. At the 'bottom' of the table was the Scilly Isles with a decline of 6.9 per cent – but from 68 to 61.1 per cent.

Value-added – conclusions

In the previous sections we have examined critically the implementation of a value-added approach to schools' achievements. Despite its intuitive appeal, largely as a reaction to awareness that raw score tables are fraught with dangers, we have argued that value-added approaches also have pitfalls. These are both conceptual and practical. But already such analyses are being undertaken, and official analyses and reports produced by the government are likely to be published from 1998 onwards.

In Chapter 1 we argued that there are eight main purposes of baseline assessment, which may be divided into two groups of four. The second category compared analyses at the level of the school and addressed accountability and improvement initiatives, or value-added. In this chapter we have revisited the evidence on the use of value-added measures.

At this time, the evidence with respect to baseline assessment is limited and will be considered in Chapter 5. By far the greatest amount of work has been carried out at secondary, and to a less extent, primary (Key Stage 2). However, these studies, publicly available data on school test and examination results, and a review of how the media treat this information, provide useful guidelines on the issues which need to be addressed.

If we return to the four issues raised by Fitz-Gibbon in her 1995 report, we can determine how well these are addressed. She argued that schemes for value-added should be:

(a) **Readily understandable.** At one level the schemes are readily understandable. Using simple, mainly single scores, it is possible to construct value-added measures. However, there are many problems with this and, as we have shown, there are sound arguments for considering different scores in the analyses. However, once this debate is opened up, teachers, let alone parents, will find the system, as a whole, less straightforward. While this is reasonable in that it reflects reality, the desire to produce simple schemes which are readily understandable will be undermined.

(b) **Statistically valid.** The evidence suggests this is achievable, but again there are caveats. It appears that simple statistical techniques based on residuals are generally as valid and useful as more complex methods, and the analyses of results suggest a coherence of methods using end of key stage data. On the other hand, there are significant effects on minorities of schools by a range of factors, including social disadvantage and gender. It is possible to include these in the analyses, but with the cost of greater complexity and possible questioning of validity with respect to 'excuses' being made for low achievement in some schools.

Furthermore, the conclusion that key stage data are sound is based on the high correlations with later attainments. Tymms (1997b) reports a correlation of 0.75 between a Key Stage 1 and Key Stage 2 score for value-added (using aggregate across English and mathematics, but not science scores). No data are presented, however, to show the concurrent reliability of the tests. Fitz-Gibbon (1997) argues that the key stage tests are improving and so supports their use. Our own data

67

suggest that there is a need for a careful analysis of reliability, and to examine why in some cases there are large variations in individual schools' performance over a period of only a year.

(c) **Not an undue burden on schools.** This appears to be achievable at KS1 and above, and indeed also at school entry.

(d) **Cost-effective.** This is more difficult to access. This may be simply addressed in terms of the actual or marginal costs associated with implementation. For example, using key stage and GCSE data, the costs of data collection are nil, but there is time needed for analysis and discussion. Baseline assessment, not yet universal, will take time away from other activities, as well as cost in terms of materials and data processing.

The larger question, however, has not yet been addressed. Will this effort be worthwhile in terms of improved outcomes of children in the future? This is less easily measured. Sound intelligence should form a good basis for schools to determine action. Alternatively, public scapegoating may harm morale and reduce effectiveness. This is an important issue, and the impact of providing value-added analyses will need to be carefully monitored over the next four years.

On balance therefore there is support for value-added analyses of school improvement, but more concern about their use in public accountability exercises. In the 'Wider Issues' chapter of her final report, Fitz-Gibbon (1997) summarises the criticisms of performance tables put forward by Peter Smith, Professor of Economics of the University of York (1995). He argues that there are a 'large number of instances of unintended behavioural consequences of the publication of performance data' (quoted in Fitz-Gibbon, p.87). He named eight:

- tunnel vision
- sub-optimisation
- myopia
- measure fixation
- misinterpretation
- misrepresentation
- gaming
- ossification.

We have touched upon some of these above, but let us consider 'gaming'. This represents 'fixing' of conditions in order that the school comes out in the best light. In the case of baseline assessment, a school would seek to be as severe as possible, to depress scores at school entry, and so appear to have a greater gain by the end of Key Stage 1. Such a process may be deliberate or less conscious in the minds of teachers and headteachers. This may be more of a concern if the measure is a checklist. When faced with a child who appears at around a cut-off, or interface between categories, the temptation may be to give the lower (worse) score. On the other hand, at the end of Key Stage 1, 'optimistic' judgements may be made in such cases.

It is important to stress that such behaviour may be more or less deliberate. When training psychologists to assess children, for example, we need to ensure that trainees are aware of their own tendencies to 'raise' or 'lower' a child's score when it is ambiguous. This is a normal part of any assessment programme implementation when there is any degree of judgement necessary.

Where public accountability and/or differential finance is dependent upon such discussions, the possibility of less benign actions must be increased. While it is true that some methods, particularly rating scales, lend themselves to the problem more than others, we consider this can be a problem with all forms of assessment. For example, anxious children or those with low self-esteem, may be helped or hindered in their performance.

A 'gaming' approach to baseline assessment may include the following:

- children assessed by the headteacher rather than the class teacher with whom they have developed a relationship;
- a 'businesslike' rather than supportive and facilitative demeanour;
- adherence to the rules do not allow any leeway for children to demonstrate their true ability;
- in case of doubt, mark down at baseline, mark up at the end of the stage.

This may be cynical, and it is not intended to criticise teachers' professionalism. It is intended to raise a very real issue when the purpose of value-added is to be public accountability rather than the school improvement.

Chapter 5

Technical quality of baseline assessment

When a new assessment method is developed it is customary for there to be an examination of its technical quality before it is used in practice. This is common sense: before using such a tool we need to know how well it works. This is true, in principle, of all fields where measurement and assessment are practised whether they be within the scope of the physical or social sciences. A newly developed electronic balance will need to be calibrated and checked over a period of time to ensure firstly that the calibrations match the standard, and secondly that its performance is maintained over time. Such development and field trials will identify inherent difficulties with the instrument, and go a long way towards pointing out errors which might arise under various conditions. For example, the balance may be insufficiently robust for certain settings. As members of the public we take such developments for granted. We expect such assessment and measurement devices to be tried and tested, and hence accurate and reliable. We do not expect to receive differing results from the same process.

Baseline assessment is no different. This is also a question of measurement and assessment, only in this instance the subjects of the process are children, and the measurement tools might be rating scales or teacher-administered tasks. The importance of the exercise, however, is no less. Judgements are to be made about the developmental status and future educational needs of the children in question. Also, as we have shown in Chapter 4, the information produced may be used as part of a process of evaluating the school.

Given these factors, it would be reasonable to expect that any baseline assessment scheme used by schools would have been subject to a rigorous development and testing programme. Potential users of an instrument, the teachers and governors who decide which approach to opt for, might reasonably assume that detailed information would be available to allow them to make judgements on the quality of each scheme. They might also assume that only those schemes which meet basic essential standards would be available anyway. This would allow them to consider methods of proven worth, but still allow them to exercise choice. Given the level of expertise it is reasonable to expect these teachers and governors to have acquired, this method makes more likely that the instrument chosen will be appropriate. This is, after all the approach of the well known kite-marking system. Furthermore, parents ought reasonably to expect that any instrument used to assess their children's progress would be fit for the purpose.

Is this the case with baseline assessment? We shall argue that the situation is one where teachers, governors and parents cannot afford to be sanguine. We shall examine the technical quality of a number of schemes, but also explore the requirements made by the School Curriculum and Assessment Authority now renamed the Qualifications and Curriculum Authority (QCA).

The SCAA accreditation criteria

The Schools Curriculum and Assessment Authority was charged with implementing a national baseline assessment programme by the Education Act 1996 (see Chapter 1). Preparation for this had been made by studies sponsored by SCAA of schemes which were in operation, and by the production in September 1996 of its *Baseline Assessment – draft proposals* (SCAA 1996b). In this document a set of key principles for the National Framework were set out. These have been reproduced in Chapter 1, Figure 1.1.

These key principles address a number of important issues but do not address directly the question of the technical quality of the instruments to be used. It could be argued that this is implicit. For example, the second bullet point stresses the principle that there should be sufficient detail to identify individual children's learning needs. However, a method might provide great detail – but be wrong! Similarly, the outcomes might contribute to value-added assessments, in that they are numerical rather than prose descriptions – but the numbers might be inaccurate.

The SCAA experimental schemes

Following the publication of the draft proposals, SCAA arranged for the evaluation of the three approaches presented as possible models in the draft proposals (see SCAA 1996c, 1996d, Caspall *et al.* 1997). These three schemes were trialled in 360 schools, 60 of which were selected as likely to have a high proportion of children learning English as an additional language. An additional 160 schools were involved in a separate trial to investigate the use of a wide range of items including aspects of personal and social development and speaking and listening.

Scheme 1 provided for assessment in relation to the *Desirable Outcomes for Children's Learning on Entering Compulsory Education* (SCAA 1996a), and gave specific criteria to identify three different levels of performance under each of the six categories. Some of these six categories were sub-divided to give 14 areas for assessment and, in each of these, criteria took the form of performance described at three different levels. Level A was close to level 1 of the National Curriculum, level B was the standard set out in the Desirable Outcomes document, and level C was below the Desirable Outcomes standard. This scheme was not well received by teachers, with only about a third of respondents reporting the criteria helpful, and only 20 per cent finding the information useful in helping them plan learning activities for children. Closer analysis of the results revealed a high degree of stability of scores across the varied areas of learning, with teachers tending to assess children very similarly across the whole range of attainments. Their judgements appeared to reflect general impressions of developmental status rather than specific attainments in each area.

Scheme 2 consisted of a checklist of early numeracy and literacy skills, providing a description of a particular skill which the teacher is asked to judge whether or not each child is able to perform, e.g. recognises letters by shape and sound, counts objects accurately, attempts to spell unfamiliar words. There were 20 such statements. About two-thirds of teachers found this format helpful, with the criteria being judged as easy to use. However, there was a general dissatisfaction with the yes–no nature of the criteria, and a view that the coverage was too narrow, with speaking and listening as well as personal and social development being regarded as important areas to assess.

Scheme 3 covered the six areas of learning from the Desirable Outcomes document, but also included the checklist of key skills from scheme 2. Teachers were simply provided with a six page booklet, and at the top of each page was a heading relating to one of the six areas, leaving the teacher to write whatever they wished about the pupil's attainments in each area. Although this approach was strongly supported by teachers, it was taking up to one hour per pupil to complete, making it impracticable for a whole class.

The conclusion from this evaluation of the three schemes was that

SCAA would develop a new set of materials, using the checklist approach, but covering personal and social development and speaking and listening as well as reading, writing and maths. The scheme should provide criteria for three different levels, but the criteria should be simple in nature so that teachers find them easy to use. This process led to the production of a SCAA scheme entitled Baseline Assessment Scales (SCAA 1997b) which are considered below. Secondly, SCAA published its National Framework for Baseline Assessment (SCAA 1997d), and it is in this document that the accreditation criteria are set out. These are reprinted in Figure 1.2 in Chapter 1.

These criteria comprise a series of sound requirements concerning the scheme itself and the process of administering the scheme. There is a reasonable match between these criteria and the key principles set out a year earlier. However, once more we can see that there are no criteria regarding the technical quality of the scheme. These are criteria governing manageability and content, and the linking of the assessment outcomes to planning and more detailed assessment as necessary. There are none which state the basic technical standards to be reached – or even that the scheme's developers should have examined this at all.

For a national framework, setting criteria for schemes to be accredited, this omission is remarkable. While many aspects of quality might be assured by following these criteria, a scheme might be approved which has technical characteristics which would be unacceptable within the professional assessment community.

The variety of approaches to baseline assessment

We have criticised the SCAA/QCA scheme for its failure to set necessary criteria with respect to technical quality. What should these be, and do schemes achieve the kinds of criteria that would be expected if an assessment procedure were to be reviewed within the research community? We shall explore these issues using five of the schemes which have provided information on their technical quality: the schemes produced in Birmingham (Birmingham City Council 1996a, 1996b, now published as *Signposts*, Birmingham City Council 1997) and Wandsworth (Wandsworth LEA 1992, Strand 1996, 1997); the PIPs scheme (Tymms and Merrill 1997, Tymms *et al*. 1995); the SCAA scales (SCAA 1997b); and the Infant Index (Desforges and Lindsay 1995a, 1995b).

The Infant Index is now also published as Baseline-*plus* (Desforges and Lindsay with Edexcel 1998). The manual for the SCAA scales contains no technical information so for this scheme we draw upon the research papers arising from the development project (SCAA 1996c, 1996d, Caspall *et al.* 1997).

Birmingham scheme

The Birmingham scheme has been in operation since 1993, and was introduced on a voluntary basis, with increasing numbers of schools becoming involved each year. Pupils are assessed through classroom observation in a wide range of contexts representing good early years practice. Assessments in 1995 were made in three areas of English (speaking and listening, reading and writing) and three areas of maths (using and applying mathematics, number, shape and space). The areas assessed and the assessment criteria are in line with the National Curriculum orders as well as with the Desirable Outcomes document. For each of the areas assessed the teachers are asked to rate each child against specified criteria. Although the original scheme did not include items on personal and social development, the latest version in use for the 1997–98 school year does, and the scheme meets the criteria outlined in the National Framework which must be met to receive accreditation from QCA. So far information on the reliability or validity of the scheme has not been published.

Teachers report that the baseline data provides an indicator of children's needs, is helpful in classroom planning and identifying those who may need further assessment, including those who may need reviewing under the Code of Practice for special educational needs. At school level it has been found to assist in curriculum planning and in the setting of targets of achievements for individuals and groups of children.

Wandsworth baseline assessment

The Wandsworth baseline assessment consists of two parts, a teacher completed checklist which involves assessing attainments in English, mathematics and science, together with an assessment of motor skills and social and emotional development, and the Linguistic Awareness for Reading Readiness test (LARR) published by NFER. Although social and emotional aspects of development are assessed they are not included in the data used to produce the baseline score (see Strand 1997).

The English and mathematics checklists use a series of questions to assess oral skills, early reading, writing, mathematical understanding and scientific development. Most questions ask the teacher to rate the pupil on a three point scale as 'developing competence', 'competent' or 'above average', although some require a simple yes–no judgement. There is a Teacher Handbook providing guidance on each section to help standardise teacher judgements across the LEA. The checklist ratings are based on teacher observations in the classroom over the whole of the first full-time term in reception. The LARR is a standardised test given to small groups of pupils taking around 20–25 minutes to complete. The test items assess whether children recognise when reading and writing are taking place, and the pupil's knowledge of technical terms such as first letter, word, etc. In this form the Wandsworth method does not meet the QCA criteria on two grounds. Firstly it takes the whole of the first term rather than being completed by the first half term, and secondly the time taken for the LARR alone is about the time recommended by the QCA for the whole of any baseline assessment, with additional time needed for completion of the checklist. However, the Wandsworth scheme has now been accredited by QCA

Analysis of the results demonstrates that the assessments produce a wide spread of scores, differentiating the range of attainments found at this age range. So far there is no information on reliability of the total package, but there are data on predictive validity using Key Stage 1 assessment results.

PIPS

Performance Indicators in Primary School (PIPS) is one of a number of assessment measures developed by the Curriculum, Evaluation and Management Centre of Durham University. The PIPS project started several years ago looking at Year 6 attainment in mathematics and the extent that this could be explained in terms of pupil ability and the schools which they attended. The project extended to look at Year 2 and Year 4 pupils with the aim of examining value-added as pupils progress through primary school, before moving to develop a baseline assessment component for use at the beginning of Infant school.

The Reception version was developed to provide a firm baseline against which progress of children can be assessed as they move through Infant school, and designed to take about 15 minutes per child, although it may take longer than this for some children. The assessment is divided into two sections, one measuring early reading skills, the other early maths skills. The assessment tasks are available as a text based system or in a multimedia computerised form. Each pupil is assessed individually by the class teacher in the first few weeks after the child has started Infant school, with no other guidance given as to how long the settling in period should be before assessment takes place. In this form PIPS does not assess personal and social development, as specified by the criteria set out by SCAA (SCAA 1997d) but, like the Wandsworth, PIPS has now been accredited.

The Reception assessment concentrates on two main areas: reading and mathematics. The reading section looks at concepts of print, with children asked to identify letters and words, before moving to letter identification and word reading tasks. Phonological awareness is also assessed. The maths section includes size, number identification and counting. The assessments are administered on a one-to-one basis by a teacher working with a child for between ten and 20 minutes, and if the child is doing well they are asked harder questions, and as they reach difficulties the assessment moves on to other items. The approach adopted by PIPS is individual teacher-based assessment using clearly specified tasks rather than the teacher rating scales of the Infant Index or Wandsworth schemes.

PIPS has been in use for a number of years, and developed on a large number of children, with data collected and analysed on further large numbers to add to the evidence on its quality.

SCAA Baseline Assessment Scales

Following the trialling of three schemes, a scheme was developed and then published by SCAA (1997b). The manual states that the scales were designed to cover aspects of the Desirable Outcomes and also some items at the standard of level 1 of the National Curriculum. The scales cover reading, writing, speaking and listening, mathematics and personal and social development. The scheme is purportedly designed to allow teachers to build upon the knowledge of the children built up over the first seven weeks in school, and no testing as such is required. However, activities are suggested in the manual to guide the teacher's judgement with directions on what to do and how to score the child's responses, and in some cases specific tasks are set out. For example, to assess phonological awareness the teacher has a resource sheet of pictures. In the first item the child is shown three pictures, told they are 'car, fork, button cup' by the teacher and asked 'Which object begins with the "c" sound?'

There are eight scales each of which may be scored at 0 to 4, and a Total score with a maximum of 32. However, the manual provides no evidence of the scores to be expected, nor of the research leading up to the publication of the scales. Data were to be published from the Autumn term 1997, according to the manual, but are not yet available at the time of writing (February 1998).

Infant Index and Baseline-plus

The final scheme to be considered in detail is that developed by ourselves. A full description of the Infant Index (Desforges and Lindsay 1995a), now published also as Baseline-*plus* (Desforges and Lindsay with Edexcel 1998), for the national baseline assessment initiative, is presented in Chapter 6.

For the present we shall use these five schemes as examples and consider the technical issues that potential users of a baseline assessment scheme should address before making their choice. There are expected to be over 80 schemes available in September 1998 according to a representative of the QCA in February 1998.

Technical quality

In the next section we shall review the schemes described briefly above. We shall focus on questions of technical quality. These are the factors which would be expected to be addressed if a measurement instrument in psychology or education were to be evaluated by the research and practitioner communities.

Face validity

The first aspect to be addressed is the least technical, but still important. Does the scheme address the factors which it might reasonably be expected to address? Does its genesis suggest a sound match between the aims of the exercise and the method itself?

For example, there was much debate in the early stages of consultation about baseline assessment regarding the range of domains to be assessed, and how these would ultimately be recorded. The SCAA criteria imply four domains, fewer for example than the National Curriculum. This may be regarded as appropriate given the age and stage in schooling of the children in question. Also, the inclusion of personal and social development was an area of debate. Although the draft proposals stated that the National Framework will encourage baseline assessment schemes to include accounts of this domain, the *Times Educational Supplement* (7 February 1997) reported that there had been proposals for only the 'three Rs' to be addressed. The *TES* stated that parents and teachers had complained about proposals to omit skills such as speaking and listening. This perception is supported by SCAA's own report of the consultation (SCAA 1997c) although this provides evidence of a desire for a broader context including assessment of fine motor skills, behaviour, willingness to help and share with others. In our view, the respondents to this consultation are correct. A scheme which was limited to just the three Rs would be too narrow.

Examination of schemes, however, indicates that this is not always addressed and some schemes are restricted. The Infant Index was designed with the active collaboration of Reception teachers (see Chapter 6) so it is perhaps not surprising that it is broad in conception. The four main areas covered by the 15 items consider literacy, maths, independent learning and social behaviour. The SCAA scheme also includes this domain, as one of eight making up the scale. On the other hand, the PIPS does not include social and emotional development. The same was true originally of the scheme developed in Birmingham. The Wandsworth scheme, on the other hand, does include social and emotional development on its checklist, but as a place for 'comment' – the same applies to motor skills. The scored items are, like PIPS within the language and maths domains, but with the addition of science.

Hence, among these five schemes there is variety in both context *per se*, and the status of the different domains with respect to the scoring of the scheme.

Reliability

There are several measures of reliability which may be examined depending upon the nature of the instrument and the purpose to which it is being put. There are two main types which are relevant for our purposes.

Inter-rater reliability. This assesses the degree to which the same result will be produced irrespective of the person administering the instrument. Variations may occur because of several reasons. These include the quality of instructions. A poor instrument may provide ambiguous directions or leave too much to the teacher (in this case) to interpret. In general, the more objective the measure, the more likely it is that two teachers will provide the same answer. A second factor concerns the administrators – they must follow the guidance in a standard fashion in order to produce comparable conditions for the child. Again, more objective measures should reduce extraneous factors, including the teachers' experience. Reliability measures are usually presented as correlation coefficients with 1.0 representing a perfect, positive correlation. In practice, with educational and psychological instruments this does not occur but the nearer to 1.0 the higher the reliability.

Inter-rater reliability for the Infant Index/Baseline-*plus* has been shown to be good at 0.89. On the other hand, no information is provided for the Wandsworth, Birmingham or SCAA schemes, so no judgements can be made.

Consistency over time. As children develop, giving the same test on two occasions some time apart, say six months, should result in different scores as the child improves in some aspects. On the other hand, assessment separated by a short period, say two to three weeks, would be expected to provide generally similar results. In addition to true development leading to changes, a test might produce different results by the inherent limitations of the procedure. For example, given a counting test, a five year old might count to 10 successfully on one day, but not on the next. Also, the teacher's judgement of a child's skills or behaviour might vary slightly from one day to another. Consequently, test–retest reliability is used to judge the degree to which a test is likely to provide consistent results over a short period of time. Again, perfect reliability is represented by 1.0.

The Infant Index has been shown to have test–retest reliability at a satisfactory level – 0.86 for the Total score. Neither the Wandsworth or Birmingham report inter-rater reliability. The PIPS is also reported to have a high level of test–retest reliability over a period of two weeks, of about 0.9 (Tymms *et al.* 1995) or 0.98, according to a later supplement. In both cases the reliability is for Total score. On the other hand, the PIPS study made use of a research assistant for the second assessment, so confounding test–retest with inter-rater reliability.

Hence, with respect to reliability, only the Infant Index provides information on two measures, and the Birmingham and Wandsworth schemes provide information on none. Where reliability has been measured, results have been satisfactory. It should be noted, however, that these good levels of reliability have been found for the total scores on the instruments. Scores for the individual items are lower and more variable. This is a common finding with instruments comprising a number of components as, essentially, the more items making up the measure, the higher reliability is likely to be.

The standardisation sample

Measurement instruments may be designed to meet either of two purposes. In the first case, a child is compared with others, usually of the same age. The most common form of this in schools is the reading test which provides a standard score. Here the teacher may compare any child's score with the distribution of others at that age.

The second purpose is to determine whether the child has achieved a specified level of skill or knowledge. A typical example is the recognition of a specific sight vocabulary, or letter sounds. In the latter case, such *criterion-referenced* measures might show all children scoring 100 per cent.

Baseline assessment schemes are, to some extent a mixture. Inherent in the structure is a norm-referenced purpose, particularly when the identification of children who might have SEN is concerned. Typically schemes have items with gradations leading to different scores. For example, the Infant Index has the following levels for its item Reading:

1 Shows an enjoyment of books, and knows how books work (front/back, left/right, top/bottom).
2 Can recognise individual words and letters in familiar context.
3 Can read from a simple story book.
0 None of the above.

In this case, the levels were produced by teachers from their experience. The question arises: are these levels correct, and what proportions of children would be expected to be at any particular level? This requires the collection of data on a group of children. This is the *standardisation sample* whose results will define the instrument's scoring criteria. The factors of relevance here are the *size* of the sample and its *make up*.

A very small sample (say one class) is clearly insufficient, and typically standardisation will be on hundreds of children at a particular age. To avoid bias (e.g. where all children are from disadvantaged backgrounds) the developers must ensure a good spread of children on key factors including gender, social disadvantage and type of school. In the case of the five instruments we are considering, the development was based on satisfactory samples. Typically, these comprised LEA age cohorts of several thousand children, and so met the size and range criteria. However, these criteria might not be met in all schemes. Again, SCAA do not make any requirements for standardisation to have been carried out, let alone the nature of the process.

Construct validity

Baseline assessment instruments have typically been developed from the opinions of experienced teachers, inspectors and psychologists, so making it likely that the items will be reasonable. However, whether it *is* the case should be investigated. One important method is to examine the degree to which the distribution of scores is reasonable. The distributions for the SCAA draft scheme are quite variable. For example, while 53 per cent of children recorded the highest score on Speaking and Listening Scale 2, this level was attained by only about 5 per cent for Reading Scale 3. Inspection of the distribution of the other items shows a good deal of variation overall. The characteristics of the Infant Index might be examined by reference to Chapter 6.

A second approach is to measure the degree to which the items discriminate. Is the instrument measuring just one factor (general development), or several (e.g. language, behaviour). Also, it is important to examine whether the items relate together in a sensible fashion if there are two or more such groupings. The evidence on the SCAA instrument suggests that each of the items is appropriate, as each correlates with the scale as a whole, at a minimum level of 0.30. An item which did not correlate would be of questionable usefulness in that scale.

A third approach is to examine the groupings of items as well as the relationship of each with the overall score. *Factor analysis* is the common approach to this. The Infant Index was subjected to this and found to have a satisfactory factor structure, as reported in the manual (Desforges and Lindsay 1995a). Further analyses of about 6,000 children from a later cohort has confirmed this finding (see Chapter 6). The factor analysis initially demonstrated that each item was related to the total score. Subsequent analyses demonstrated two main factors: Basic Skills and Independent Learning. This is a coherent structure.

Predictive validity

Construct validity essentially measures the instrument as it is at a particular time. In addition we would wish to discover the degree to which a baseline assessment instrument predicted later development, at the end of the Reception year, or the end of Key Stage 1, for example. This investigation is more problematic for two reasons – one practical, the other conceptual.

Firstly, such evaluation requires time. The development of a scale would normally build this in. This has recurred with the Infant Index, PIPS and Wandsworth schemes. The SCAA scheme is too new. Secondly, there is a conceptual dilemma known as the *paradox of prediction*. We would like a test to show a very high predictive power. For example, if we have our blood pressure measured we assume that the prediction from the instrument is very highly correlated with actually having high blood pressure. But this is a *concurrent* measure. To predict, later coronary disease, on the basis of high blood pressure at age 25 years, is of a different order – other factors such as diet and exercise subsequently will matter. The same applies in education.

Suppose all the children identified as being 'at risk' were then provided with top quality and highly effective intervention. At the end of Key Stage 1 these children would score well on the assessment. The result is to *reduce* the apparent predictive power of the baseline assessment. The paradox is this: we use baseline assessment to identify children so that we prevent later problems; to be certain the correct children are identified we need a valid instrument; but if the instrument is valid and we act appropriately, the predictive power of the baseline assessment will *appear* lower than it really is. Hence, the examination of instruments including baseline assessment for predictive validity is fraught. It would still be expected, however, that this issue would be addressed in normal test construction.

The PIPS scheme reports high correlations with reading and maths at the end of the Reception year (e.g. Total score correlated 0.67 with maths and 0.72 with reading for n = 1,738 children). The correlations between PIPS and Key Stage 1 assessments were lower, e.g. English and maths assessments combined was 0.62 (Tymms 1997a). These scores indicate that the PIPS is a reasonable predictor of later performance, although Tymms points out that the predictability of children is not uniform. Whereas those scoring at the top end (>70) have a very high chance of gaining level 3 at Key Stage 1, the outcomes for those scoring below 30 on PIPS are much more variable.

Analyses of the predictive validity of the Infant Index compared its predictive power over the longer period, to the end of Key Stage 1. Correlation coefficients for the Total score and the Basic Skills subscale with Key Stage 1 assessments of about 330 children were 0.35, and 0.34 respectively. Further information is provided in Chapter 6. These coefficients are highly significant, but moderate in size. A further factor in this set of comparisons is the scoring system of the Key Stage 1 assessments, being a limited range of 0 to 3. This has the effect of reducing correlations – Tymms used 8 point scales in his analyses, which should lead to increased size of correlation coefficients. Nevertheless, while the results suggest the Infant Index has predictive validity, there is also a warning that its predictive power over two to three years is only moderate.

The Wandsworth scheme also has information on its validity against Key Stage 1 results. Higher correlations are reported, with an average of 0.60. This might be for several reasons. Firstly, the Wandsworth scheme includes a reading test (the LARR) which lengthens the administration time, but provides a greater range of scores. Secondly, the analysis was restricted to English and maths scores, plus the LARR. Thirdly, the Key Stage 1 results were rescaled from a 4 point to a 6 point scale.

Predictive validity, therefore, is a problematic area, but some of the schemes have not only attempted to measure it, but have also reported satisfactory levels. Those scales which are limited to 'academic' scores tend to show higher correlations, not surprising as the skills are more directly related. Also, using 6 or 8 point scales for Key Stage 1 data also improves the correlations. However, not all schemes have this information and, again, SCAA have not required accredited schemes to demonstrate either a satisfactory level of predictive validity or even that this has been investigated.

Characteristics of subgroups

Any instrument may discriminate between individuals in one of two ways. The first is proper and valid, namely to distinguish individuals on the overt criteria of the test. For example, a driving test should discriminate successfully between competent drivers and those not competent. The second, improper discrimination occurs when subgroups are distinguished on *irrelevant* criteria. For example, if proportionately more taller than shorter candidates passed the test, this would raise questions about its validity. This is an equal opportunities issue (Wolfendale 1998).

It is normally expected, therefore, in developing instruments that such discriminations are researched – note the term 'discrimination' is used in its technical, non-prejudicial sense. In the case of baseline assessment, therefore, we need also to examine the degree to which schemes discriminate subgroups, and then judge whether these distinctions are valid and helpful, or invalid, and unhelpful, even prejudicial.

Gender

There is a common finding among our five schemes that boys are performing at a lower level than girls. This was found for the PIPS, Wandsworth scheme, Infant Index and Birmingham scheme (although the latter does not provide evidence that this was statistically significant). No gender analysis is provided for the SCAA. Interestingly, Strand (1997) has also shown that girls make better progress over Key Stage 1 than boys.

Pre-school experience

It might be expected that children who had been to nursery school or other pre-school provision would perform better on baseline assessment than those who had not had such experiences. The Birmingham report suggests that children attending LEA nursery school or classes performed better than those who had no experience, or had attended playgroups or day nurseries. However, the numbers involved were low, and no statistical analyses were carried out. The PIPS data suggest children who had attended either nurseries or playgroups performed a little better than those who had not. The Infant Index showed no difference between types of pre-school provision, but those who had not attended any such provision scored lowest. The Wandsworth scheme did not differentiate the pre-school provision, but also found a significant effect. This superiority was maintained to the end of Key Stage 1.

Ethnic status and English as an additional language

The results for the Infant Index are shown in the next chapter, see Table 6.5. White, Black Caribbean and Chinese children scored at a comparable level, but children of Pakistani or Bangladeshi origin scored significantly lower. The Birmingham scale shows similar differences by ethnic status, but no statistical analyses were performed to investigate their significance. The Infant Index revealed a similar pattern when mother tongue was compared – children whose first language is Urdu or Bengali score at lower levels than those for whom English is the first language (see Table 6.6 in Chapter 6).

The Wandsworth scheme does not report analyses between ethnic groups, or specific family language, but does report lower scores among those children for whom English was an additional language.

Age effects

Children enter school at different points in the year according to LEA practice. Hence, while some might be in Reception for three terms, others might be present for only two or one term or even have no Reception experience. SCAA requires that baseline assessment is administered within seven weeks after school entry. This results in children potentially having a wide range of ages at this time. Where children enter in the term in which they are aged five, the spread will be small – about four months. For example, Autumn term entrants assessed towards the end of October will range from about four years ten months to five years two months. However, in a school where *all* children enter in September, children whose birthday is in August will only be about four years two months at assessment.

Sheffield has the former policy; children were assessed in the term in which they were five. Analyses of the Infant Index results found no age effects. That is, comparable scores were achieved by each of the three terms' entrants. The PIPS scheme, on the other hand, reports an age effect. Children with birthdays in July and August recorded lower scores than those born in September and October. This trend was shown over the year, and was also found in the Wandsworth and Birmingham data. No information is available on the SCAA scheme, as it was trialled at only one admission point, in January.

Social disadvantage

No information is available on the SCAA scheme, but the other four all report that socially disadvantaged children tend to have lower scores. Also, Strand (1997) reports that these children as a group make worse progress over Key Stage 1, and hence fall further behind.

Taking these five characteristics as a whole, it is clear that any baseline assessment scheme must address each of them. For example, the different levels achieved by children for whom English is a first language indicates that their general development, as measured on baseline assessment schemes examined here, was lower. This does not, however, imply these children are inherently less able, or that they will continue to score at this level. On the contrary, Strand (1997) has produced evidence to indicate that children for whom English was an additional language made good progress to the end of Key Stage 1, by which time they achieved scores on

Key Stage 1 assessments comparable to those achieved by monolingual English-speaking children. On the other hand, socially disadvantaged children not only tend to score lower at school entry, they also tend to make less progress and so fall further behind.

Conclusions

We have focused primarily on five schemes to explore the issue of technical quality of baseline assessment. Within these schemes, the information available, and the analyses carried out, are varied. In general, there are a number of positive indicators about the schemes, but also some gaps. For example, while some reports suggest differences between subgroups, no statistical analysis is provided to back up the statements. It should be noted that these schemes were chosen as examples because information about their technical quality was available. What information will be available on the rest of the 80 or so schemes that are, or are due to be accredited? And what will be the standard of the technical quality of the schemes?

We have indicated throughout this chapter that SCAA has not required schemes to demonstrate particular standards with respect to technical quality. Not only that, the accreditation criteria do not ever require that such investigations be carried out. For a scheme which is to be applied, by force of law, to all schools with five-year-old children this is remarkable. If the schemes do not have adequate quality two effects will occur, related to the two main areas of purpose determined by SCAA.

In the first case, children will be misclassified and their needs misunderstood. This could result in children being placed on the SEN register inappropriately, and being made subject to unnecessary intervention. Equally, they could lose out on the experiences other children are receiving. Secondly, such errors will have an effect on the baseline measure at the school level. When the value-added analysis is undertaken after the Key Stage 1 results, this also will be subject to error.

At present, therefore, we have a system about to be implemented across the country that has no quality assurance built in to ensure that the risks of these two eventualities are reduced. Some schemes have information which allows headteachers, governors and Reception teachers to make judgements, but the SCAA accreditation is not sufficient. We might wonder whether this is the standard of practice to which it is reasonable to expose our young children.

Chapter 6

Development of the Infant Index and Baseline-*plus*

Introduction

The Infant Index is a teacher rating scale designed for use with Reception class pupils entering Infant school, for completion within the first half term of school entry. It is a system for assessing all children, and provides a profile of attainments in the areas of literacy skills, maths, social behaviour (including language skills), and independent learning skills. It provides structured information on attainment levels in basic skill areas as well as on behaviours important for independent and group learning within an Infant classroom.

The information obtained can be used for a variety of purposes. Each child's attainments can be compared against those of the others coming into the school and, by linking with the structure of the National Curriculum core subjects, the information can be used to help classroom organisation to ensure appropriate learning experiences for individuals or groups of pupils. The numerical scores provided by the profiles allow the Infant Index to be used as a general screening instrument which identifies children who may be at risk of having, or developing, special educational needs.

From September 1998, all maintained primary schools in England will be required to carry out baseline assessment on all pupils entering Infant school, using a scheme accredited by the Qualifications and Curriculum Authority. The Infant Index meets the requirements of the criteria set out by the QCA, and a version of the Infant Index, Baseline-*plus* (Desforges and Lindsay with Edexcel 1998) has been formally accredited for use by schools. It offers score sheets capable of being read by an optical mark reader, together with a computerised data analysis service.

The *Code of Practice on the Identification and Assessment of Special Educational Needs* (DfE 1994) offers guidance to schools on their responsibilities towards pupils with special educational needs as set out in

Part 3 of the 1993 Education Act. The Infant Index will help schools working with pupils at one of the first three stages of school-based assessment and provision for special educational needs.

Developing the Infant Index

The Infant Index predates the current interest in baseline assessment arising from the statutory requirements placed on schools to carry out an assessment on all pupils starting Infant school. The initial stimulus for the development came from a group of headteachers of inner city infant schools, who in 1991 were concerned at the possibility of Key Stage 1 National Curriculum assessment results being published in league tables. They wanted to consider the possibility of using a baseline assessment measure against which progress during Key Stage 1 could be assessed, as well as wanting to revisit the issues around the early identification of, and early intervention with, pupils at risk of having special educational needs.

At the beginning of this project it was agreed that we would take a research-based approach, using the expertise of different professional groups interested in the issues around baseline assessment. A small group was set up comprising a headteacher, an experienced deputy headteacher, two advisory teachers for National Curriculum Assessment (Primary), a special needs teacher currently a university research worker, and ourselves. This team of seven agreed that we should aim to devise a baseline assessment procedure in the form of a simple checklist that is linked directly to the National Curriculum and reflects important skills necessary for school-based learning. It quickly became clear that an approach using a teacher rating scale would be appropriate, and a major influence was the work carried out by one of the team some ten years earlier in developing the Infant Rating Scale (Lindsay 1981). The plan was to draw up a pilot scale, conduct evaluative studies to further refine the scale and to examine its technical qualities. The team was committed to a prolonged development phase, and realised that it had embarked on a project that would take several years, going through several cycles of development, implementation, evaluation and review.

Technical issues

Over the last twenty years many LEAs have decided to develop programmes of early identification, and gathered groups of professionals, usually teachers, advisers and psychologists, to devise a suitable method.

These projects have often been limited to developing an instrument for an agreed purpose, with little in the way of evaluative research to look at issues of reliability, validity and fitness for the purpose. It is as though the professional views of those concerned are sufficient to develop an appropriate checklist or screening device. The purpose is usually to identify difficulties, and contribute to planning the future education of pupils. These are major decisions, and instruments of less than satisfactory quality may lead to significant errors, possibly contributing to harmful outcomes for children. From the beginning of the project there was agreement that these technical issues should be addressed, and data presented in a form which helped users interpret the significance of the results, and raise an awareness of the limitations of the data.

Two important issues in any form of assessment are those of reliability and validity (see Chapter 5). Reliability is a measure of the accuracy of the instrument, and the errors of measurement associated with it. There are a number of ways of considering reliability and the Infant Index used two approaches. One, the test–retest reliability involves the same assessor using the instrument on the same children on two occasions over a short time period and looking at how similar the scores are. Inter-rater reliability involves two people independently rating the same children, and again comparing the scores. The results of this exercise are reported below.

Validity is a consideration of whether the instrument actually measures what it sets out to measure. Validity was assessed in a number of ways – construct validity, face validity and predictive validity. Details of the methods and the results are reported below.

Initial phase

A group of 16 infant schools was chosen to reflect the full range of communities within one LEA, and included schools from large council estates, inner city areas and more affluent suburban areas. Schools were rated on a scale of disadvantage (using free school meals as the indicator) and the sample chosen to reflect low, medium and high disadvantage. In addition, some schools were chosen because of the high proportion of children from ethnic minority backgrounds. The headteachers of the schools selected agreed to allow their reception class teachers to take part, and these teachers were asked:

> 'What ten things do you expect a child to be able to do at infant school entry in order to reach National Curriculum level 2 at the end of key stage 1, at age 7?'

No further guidance was given. We were aware that teachers would give a variety of views, and this diversity was welcomed. It was useful to see what teachers regarded as important.

In theory, as 16 teachers were involved it would have been possible to get 160 different items. In practice these items were found to cluster round key areas. Many items related to language skills – retell a story, good vocabulary, naming shapes, recognising some letters and words. Some related to number skills – count to ten, recognise numbers to ten. Other areas highlighted by teachers were concerned with social development – able to sit still and listen, able to dress themselves, be well adjusted enough socially to enjoy school, and to be able to work alone or in small groups without the need for constant adult attention.

These responses were then analysed according to the National Curriculum. Items were matched against attainment targets wherever possible. For example, many items related to language skills: retell a story, vocabulary (e.g. able to name primary colours and basic shapes such as circle, square or triangle; recognise some letters and words). Some related to number skills: count to ten, simple sorting activities, recognising numbers to ten. Others highlighted areas of independent learning skills and of personal and social development that were not part of the National Curriculum.

A total of 15 areas were identified from the teachers' responses, and for each one, three differing levels were drawn up. For example, in relation to reading:

Shows an enjoyment of books, and knows how books work (front/back, left/right, top/bottom) – item level 1
Can recognise individual words or letters in familiar context – item level 2
Can read from a simple story book – item level 3
None of the above – item level 0.

This initial profile was piloted in the same group of 16 schools, with every fourth child who started school in September 1992 taking part. Teachers were asked to complete the profile between the period four weeks after the start of term and the October half term (October 1992). It was felt that the four weeks would give sufficient time for the teacher to get to know the children, and allow the pupils time to settle into school and get over any short-term emotional difficulties. Completion before half term would give a profile of entry skills. In addition to completing the profile the teachers were asked to comment on the individual questions and on the profiles as a whole.

The results revealed a good deal of support for the profile, but amendments were required to clarify the meaning of some items, and the sequence of others needed some changes. This revised profile was then circulated to all schools in the LEA, with a request for them to complete a 1 in 4 sample of all pupils starting school in January 1993, and again in September 1993, a total of over 900 pupils. The results were placed on computer and analysed. As a result of this analysis some items were modified. During this time the National Curriculum was revised, leading to revision of some items in the area of literacy skills. Further changes to the wording of some items were made following comments from teachers completing the profile. The final version was then used on a 1 in 3 sample of children starting school in September 1994, a further 500 pupils.

The sampling technique used, involving a random sample from more than 90 per cent of the schools with an infant intake in the LEA, ensured a standardisation sample reflecting the gender, ethnic and socio-economic composition of the LEA.

Structure of the Infant Index

The initial grouping of the items into subscales was done on the basis of a common-sense view. Four subscales were used: language and literacy, mathematical skills, social behaviour and independent learning. However, factor analysis of the results (see Table 6.1) indicated that the language items loaded with the social behaviour items rather than with literacy skills, and as a result the four subscales used were: literacy skills, mathematical skills, social behaviour (including language), and independent learning skills. The changes made following factor analysis indicate the importance of careful evaluation, as well as professional opinion when developing assessment instruments (see Desforges and Lindsay 1995b for further discussion). The structure of the Infant Index is shown in Figure 6.1.

Reliability

There are several types of reliability, but not all are appropriate for the Infant Index. A sample of 74 children from five schools was used to obtain an inter-rater reliability (comparison of the rating of the same children by different adults, each completed the Infant Index independently). There are difficulties with this, as infant children usually have only one class teacher who knows the child well enough to complete the Infant Index. In four schools, involving 55 pupils, both the class teacher and a non-teaching assistant who spent significant amounts of time in the class, each independently completed the Infant Index on the same children. The correlation for the whole score was 0.89. A further sample, using two reception classes each with two teachers job sharing, gave a correlation of 0.91.

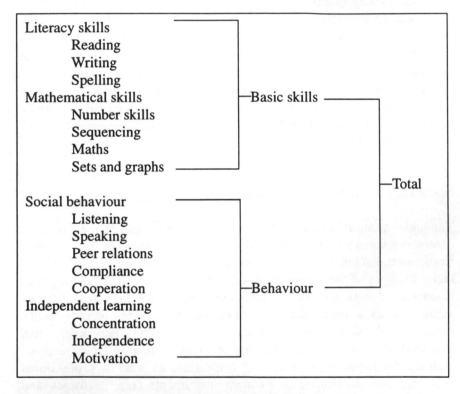

Figure 6.1 The structures of the Infant Index and Baseline-*plus*

A further four schools were used to obtain test–retest reliability coefficients, where the Infant Index was completed twice on each child with a 14 day interval between. The first Index was collected by the headteacher immediately after completion, and the class teachers had no records of the results. Fourteen days later supply cover was provided and the teachers again completed the Index on the same children. The test–retest correlation was 0.86.

Validity

Validity can be assessed in a number of different ways. The Infant Index was constructed using the views of informed professionals to select items that they judged as related to successful school learning, and as a result could be said to have a high face validity. Analysis of the results indicates highly significant differences in scores achieved by boys and by girls, with girls scoring significantly higher on both basic skills and behaviour. This is a common finding in many assessment instruments, and can be taken as further evidence of the validity of the Infant Index. The Index has a coherent internal structure, as indicated by the factor analysis, showing that the items cluster around two factors, basic skills and social behaviour (Desforges and Lindsay 1995a). Further development of the Infant Index, with a slight modification to two items, produced a very similar factor matrix on a full cohort of 5,918 Sheffield school entrants during 1996–7 (see Table 6.1). Indeed, the items are more strongly associated with one or other factor.

Table 6.1 Factor analysis of the Infant Index/Baseline-*plus*

Item	Loading Factor 1	Loading Factor 2
Reading	**0.76**	0.23
Writing	**0.74**	0.24
Spelling	**0.80**	0.25
Number skills	**0.76**	0.25
Sequencing	**0.72**	0.24
Maths	**0.72**	0.30
Sets and graphs	**0.66**	0.30
Listening	0.37	**0.72**
Speaking	0.44	**0.59**
Peer relationships	0.27	**0.74**
Compliance	0.16	**0.77**
Cooperation	0.28	**0.74**
Concentration/attention	0.40	**0.68**
Independence/self-help	0.11	**0.51**
Motivation	0.25	**0.71**

N = 5918

Predictive validity looks at how accurately the Infant Index can predict future educational attainments. So far two studies have taken place, but because of the three year time gap between completing the Index and comparing scores with current attainments, the data refer to the earlier pilot version rather than to the refined version of the Infant Index. One study has looked at the link between Infant Index scores and National Curriculum results at the end of Key Stage 1. The results are summarised in Table 6.2. It can be seen that the correlations are modest in size, from 0.31 to 0.37, but statistically highly significant. It should be noted that there is no information available on the reliability of the National Curriculum results, and there is some evidence that for example, the scores from the reading standard assessment task (SAT) do not relate closely to scores obtained on standardised reading tests given within a few days of the SAT (see Chapter 4). A further difficulty is that National Curriculum scores only give outcomes in terms of levels, with only four scores possible. More recent work has used a six point scoring by making use of the level 2 a, b or c grades awarded on the literacy tasks. Extending the range of scores allows for the possibility of higher correlations than simply using a four point scale.

Table 6.2 Correlation of Infant Index scores with Key Stage 1 assessment

Key Stage 1	Infant Index Scores		
	Total	Basic skills	Behaviour
Reading	0.31	0.32	0.23
English	0.33	0.33	0.28
Spelling	0.32	0.30	0.28
Writing	0.31	0.30	0.25
Mathematics	0.37	0.34	0.33
Science	0.28	0.28	0.23
Total	0.35	0.34	0.29

N = 328–335 all significant at 0.0001 level

A further study was carried out using the September 1993 pilot version of the Infant Index, where the Infant Index scores were matched with scores obtained on a non-verbal reasoning test and the NFER-Nelson group reading test 6–12. Scores were matched for 340 pupils out of the 444 pupils in the original cohort (see Morissey 1997). There were no significant differences in Infant Index scores between the 340 whose scores were matched, and the 104 who were not traced. Table 6.3 summarises the results, where it can be seen that the correlations are highest for Total score and basic skills scores with non-verbal reasoning scores. A further analysis indicated that the correlations were higher for boys than girls.

Table 6.3 Correlation of Infant Index scores and Year 3 non-verbal reasoning and group reading scores

Infant Index	Year 3 non-verbal reasoning	Year 3 group reading
Total score	0.38	0.30
Basic skills	0.40	0.30
Behaviour	0.30	0.25

All significant at 0.0001 level

An alternative way of looking at the links between the two scores is to consider how efficient the Infant Index is at identifying children into the 'at risk' or 'not at risk' category. Using the scores on the non-verbal reasoning test, 75 per cent of pupils were correctly categorised (see Table 6.4). This fell to 66 per cent using the scores on the group reading test. Again, from a statistical point of view all the associations are highly significant, but are modest in size. This is not unexpected as some children with good non-verbal reasoning may have limited skills on school entry, but be capable of good progress. The evidence from Wandsworth (Strand 1997) indicates this pattern for children for whom English is an additional language.

Of course one difficulty with these types of studies is that the data from the Infant Index scores are known to teachers, and used by them to identify children at risk, and to put in place programmes which will address those difficulties. If this early intervention is successful, then the children concerned should be scoring at a higher level three years later, and hence overturning the prediction made as a result of the earlier score. Only if the teachers are unaware of the original score, and do not plan any interventions based on it could we accurately look at the predictive power. There are serious moral concerns with such approaches, and the aim of education is to maximise the attainments of all children.

However, the results of the studies reported here lead to the conclusion that the pilot Infant Index has a coherent structure, satisfactory reliability, but its ability to predict later educational outcomes, while highly significant, is only moderate. Whilst the Infant Index provides accurate information about children's current learning needs, caution needs to be exercised when attempting to use it to predict future learning outcomes three or more years after it is administered. Further studies will be undertaken on the final version of the Infant Index, which may be expected to lead to improvements in size of correlations, but may still be of a relatively modest nature.

Table 6.4 Frequencies of pupils correctly classified as 'at risk' or 'not at risk' by Infant Index using scores on non-verbal reasoning at 7+ as the criterion measure

	At or below 20th centile on non-verbal reasoning	Above 20th centile on non-verbal reasoning	Total
At or below 20th centile on Infant Index	7%	10%	17%
Above 20th centile on Infant Index	14%	69%	83%
Total	21%	79%	100%

Feedback from teachers

As noted earlier, the form and content of the Index was from the start shaped by teacher views. In 1996, following the use of the Infant Index on all children entering Infant school, teachers were asked for feedback using a questionnaire during the Summer term, after they had completed record sheets on a complete cohort. Teachers from 57 schools out of the 114 involved responded. Most felt that 15–25 minutes per child was needed to complete the assessment, and that they got faster as they became more familiar with the structure of the Infant Index. There were some difficulties in keeping other pupils usefully occupied when the teacher was focusing on particular skills, especially in the maths domain, and the presence of an extra adult was seen as helpful. Broadly, teachers were reasonably happy about interpreting the statements, with many schools organising opportunities for teachers to liaise with colleagues before making assessments, and in some cases carrying out joint assessments. In schools with only one reception teacher there was a request for opportunities to meet with colleagues from other schools to discuss interpretation of statements and issues of moderation. Some schools carried out more detailed assessments using their own schemes and transferred information to the Infant Index records. Overall teachers were satisfied with the Infant Index and the demands made on them, and used the information gathered to inform classroom planning.

Using the Infant Index

The most recent standardisation used data from more than 6,000 pupils. These were analysed to provide frequency charts for item, subscale, composite scale and Total scores. In this way raw scores can be converted into centile scores, providing norm referenced data, which can be used to identify the two per cent of children that might be considered to be at high risk of having marked problems with school-based learning, and the further 18 per cent of children that might be at moderate risk, requiring extra attention, more careful monitoring and carefully focused interventions as recommended in the Code of Practice (DfE 1994).

The data can be analysed to look at how particular groups of children have scored on the Infant Index. Tables 6.5 and 6.6 give information on scores according to ethnic status and community language. In summary, pupils of Bangladeshi and Pakistani heritage score at a significantly lower level than white European and African-Caribbean pupils. These findings are similar to those from other areas using different baseline assessment instruments, and raise some fundamental issues.

Table 6.5 Mean Infant Index scores by ethnicity

Ethnic group	Basic skills	Behaviour	Total score	Number of individuals
White	10.39	17.80	28.14	5282
Black African	6.38	15.83	22.00	18
African-Caribbean	10.59	17.67	28.13	87
Black Other	9.22	17.39	26.47	71
Indian	8.28	18.00	26.28	7
Pakistani	5.68	14.40	20.00	295
Bangladeshi	4.89	14.12	18.89	39
Chinese	11.23	17.29	28.52	17

Table 6.6 Mean Infant Index scores by mother tongue

Mother tongue	Basic skills	Behaviour	Total score	Number of individuals
English	10.35	17.81	28.13	5488
Urdu	5.71	14.38	20.01	289
Bengali	4.53	13.84	18.25	39
Arabic	8.00	15.00	23.00	25
Somali	5.86	14.95	20.63	22
Cantonese	11.50	16.28	27.78	14

There is evidence that by the end of junior school and into the early years of secondary school African-Caribbean pupils are scoring lower than white pupils. The finding that they are entering infant school with levels of skills and attainments similar to those of white pupils suggests that schools are not meeting the educational needs of these pupils as well as they are meeting the needs of white pupils.

There is also an important point arising from the finding that pupils of Bangladeshi and Pakistani heritage are scoring at significantly lower levels than other ethnic groups. One interpretation is that the assessment instrument is biased against them, and insofar as the Infant Index focuses on language skills in English, it does discriminate against pupils whose mother tongue is not English, and who enter school at a very early stage of learning English as a second language. However, the learning environment of the school is one where English is the medium of instruction and most transactions between pupils and teachers are through the medium of English. The results of baseline assessment therefore draw attention to the learning needs of, and the resource implications for, these pupils, and allow questions to be posed about how the education system can respond to the needs of these pupils to ensure they can learn at an appropriate rate. It should be noted that the lower scores of these two groups are not just in the area of basic skills, but also in the areas of independent learning and social behaviour. It is of interest that the QCA criteria for baseline assessment (SCAA 1997d) specify that speaking and listening, reading and writing must establish children's fluency in English, but 'may, as appropriate use English, the child's preferred language, or a combination of both to assess attainment in mathematics, personal and social development and any other area covered by the scheme'.

Finally, the data can be used to allow schools to compare their own performance with the aggregated data from the whole LEA. Figure 6.2

summarises some of these differences, showing a wide spread of mean scores for schools, the lowest having a mean total score of 16, the highest a mean total score of 36. These differences raise questions about the use of baseline data to allocate certain elements of funding on the basis of direct education measures rather than on proxy indicators of socio-economic status such as free school meals.

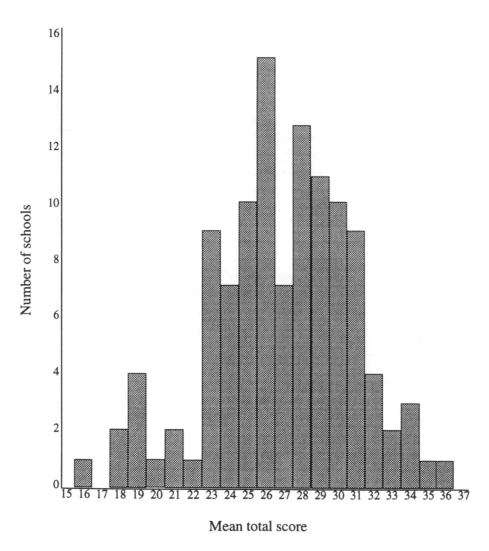

Figure 6.2 Number of schools by mean Infant Index total score

Using the Infant Index as an evaluation instrument

Community based services for pre-school children and their parents aim to prevent, identify or modify conditions that might impede development and contribute to subsequent educational difficulties. There are problems in evaluating these community based support programmes, with no simple outcome measure for the success of these initiatives. The ideal outcome measure would be widely available, cheap to administer, reliable, valid, sensitive to pre-school factors likely to affect educational progress and capable of measuring changes of educational significance on a community-wide scale. The Infant Index offers opportunities for such work, and a pilot study has been carried out to ascertain whether Infant Index scores gathered by schools could be matched to health data routinely available from community health care (see Rigby *et al.* 1997).

The study was based on the matching of two data sets collected in Sheffield for children born in the academic year spanning 1991 and 1992. The study, and in particular the method of ensuring anonymisation, were approved by the Local Research Ethics Committee. The health data set included data on breast feeding, maternal age, baby's weight gain, parity, state of housing repair, and score on the Edinburgh Postnatal Depression Scale.

It was possible to match 75 per cent of the cohort, and analysis of the Infant Index scores of the matched and unmatched groups indicated no systematic differences between the two groups. Statistical analysis explored associations between the Infant Index scores coded as poor (the bottom 20 per cent, to coincide with the percentage of the school population likely to have learning difficulties, as defined by the Code of Practice, at some time in their school career), versus good (the remaining 80 per cent of the population). The statistical associations between the various health and social factors and the Infant Index were calculated as odds ratios (odds of a poor versus a good outcome) with 95 per cent confidence intervals.

The results showed that boys were twice as likely as girls to have a poor Infant Index score, confirming the results of many other studies. Another strong predictor of outcome was birthweight, children weighing less than 2.5 kgs at birth were more likely to have a poor outcome on the Infant Index score than those weighing more than 2.5 kgs. Other significant factors were number of siblings (with those having four or more siblings having a much greater chance of achieving a low score on the Infant Index), poor housing, bottle feeding at three months, and postnatal depression.

This study shows that biological and social factors assessed in the first month of life, and known to have associations with developmental and educational outcomes, showed significant associations with Infant Index scores at Infant school entry. Using routinely collected educational data to assess the effects of early interventions with children and families at risk would make evaluation of these interventions cheaper and more efficient in terms of professional time, and demonstrates the cost-effectiveness of inter-agency working .

Baseline-*plus*

The Infant Index has been the subject of a continuing research project and information is now available on two whole cohorts of children entering school in Sheffield (almost 12,000 in total). As a preparation for city wide use, a version was developed for use by an optical mark reader. This allows easy marking and analysis of scores for individuals, and also for school or LEA data as a whole. This version has now been released as Baseline-*plus* (Desforges and Lindsay with Edexcel 1998), and has been accredited by the QCA for use by schools as part of the national baseline assessment programme.

Chapter 7

Early identification and the Code of Practice

Identification of special educational needs is the first stage in the process of determining what provision a child might require. Identification might be seen as a precursor to assessment. In this approach, identification is a more general, less precise determination. Rather, it is a process whereby indications are noted, hunches are explored, and hypotheses are formulated. Identification is, therefore, a stage when the focus is on the child as a whole, while the assessment is concerned with more detailed analysis of the components of the child's particular combination of skills, knowledge and difficulties.

We shall adopt this distinction as a working model, but it is important to stress that this is only a device to aid our consideration of these processes. It could be argued, for example, that identification actually *follows* assessment, and that it is once a child's needs have been assessed and set down that they as individuals have been identified. We prefer the former approach, however, as this follows the natural progression of events, and also is the approach taken in the *Code of Practice on the Identification and Assessment of Special Educational Needs* (DfE 1994).

The importance of identifying children's SEN at an early stage was highlighted in the report of the Bullock Committee *A Language for Life* (DES 1975). This addressed the question of literacy and language development in general, but included a chapter on early identification. At that time, some authorities had screening programmes which attempted to identify children with literacy difficulties, but these tended to be in the early Junior years, when children were seven to nine years of age. The Bullock Committee explored approaches available at that time, and advocated that earlier identification was advisable, to pick up children before they developed major difficulties, before they 'failed' to learn to read. The focus should be on the identification of children 'at risk'.

The Education Act 1993 and the Code of Practice

The Education Act 1993 built upon the evidence which had been gathered about the operation of the 1981 Act. There were a number of concerns with how the system had been working, including major disparities between LEAs in the percentages of children with statements, and the time which the statutory assessment process took. One of the concerns expressed by practitioners and parents was the lack of guidance from the Department for Education, so resulting in each LEA devising its own methods. For example, each authority determined the forms which would be completed, or indeed whether there were forms at all. The 1981 Act had specified the advice which was required (educational, medical and psychological were mandatory) and Circular 22/89 had given guidance on the areas to address, but the general approach was to require LEAs to develop their own systems. The shortcomings in this process were identified both by the House of Commons Select Committee (1987) and the report of the Audit Commission and Her Majesty's Inspectors (1992).

The 1993 Act, therefore, included a requirement that the Secretary of State should issue a Code of Practice which would give guidance to LEAs and governing bodies of all maintained schools on their responsibilities towards all children with SEN. Published in 1994, the Code has been welcomed and found helpful by professionals working in the field, although it does have limitations as we shall come on to examine. This was the first comprehensive approach to identification and assessment produced by the Department for Education. It was accompanied by separate documents including six Circulars and *Pupils with Problems* and replaced the DES Circular 22/89 mentioned above, the Welsh Office equivalent, and other related documents. The Code of Practice included as an appendix the Statutory Instrument 1994 No. 1047 The Education (Special Educational Needs) Regulations 1994.

One confusion which needs to be cleared at the outset is that the Code of Practice is *not* the law, it is not mandatory. Rather, as stated in paragraph 6 of the Foreword:

> All those to whom the Code applies have a statutory duty to have regard to it; they must not ignore it.

Hence, the key phrase is 'have regard to' the Code. This is spelled out in the next paragraph which suggests that the effect of having regard to the Code 'might vary according to circumstances and over time' (paragraph 7). Of particular relevance to the present discussion is the statement:

Thus, for example, schools' governing bodies and head teachers should reflect, in the light of the Code, on the way in which schools identify, assess and make provision for children with special educational needs. In that way, this will be having regard to the Code. But the detail of what they decide to do might vary according to the size, organisation, location and pupil population of the school. (DfE 1994, p.ii)

The Code is to be seen as an important set of guidance. It does not lay down exact, unalterable requirements. This has obvious benefits. The situation in an infant school of fewer than 100 children is clearly different from that of a very large secondary school. The former will allow much firsthand knowledge of all children by the headteacher, and probably all staff. The size of the secondary school will not allow every child to be known by all staff, and hence additional mechanisms and modes of communication are necessary. With respect to identification, for example, a secondary school would need to consult all the staff teaching the child.

Our focus is on the early years of schooling, and that will guide the rest of our discussion about the Code. It is necessary, however, to appreciate that the Code is not definitive. While this might not matter too much at the more mundane level of deciding the exact format of reports, there are more substantial matters to consider when, for example, the criteria for deciding to make a statutory assessment are the points at issue.

The five-stage model

The Code of Practice is explicit with respect to early identification. It argues that its importance, along with that of assessment and provision for any child who may have SEN cannot be overemphasised.

The earlier action is taken, the more responsive the child is likely to be, and the more readily can intervention be made without undue disruption to the organisation of the school including the delivery of the curriculum for that particular child. (DfE 1994, para. 2.16)

This rationale has two components. Firstly, early intervention is advisable as the child will be more responsive. This is a view which is not to be taken without challenge. In some cases, early identification and provision have clear benefits and are unquestionable in their necessity. These include certain metabolic disorders which might lead to intellectual or physical impairment, but whose effects can be minimised or defeated by therapies including drugs or special diets. But other children develop at a slower rate. Also, the normal range of development at any age is quite wide, so the designation that a child has a difficulty is not always straightforward. Finally, in some cases intervention might be more appropriate later, when a child has a greater maturity and can bring other personal strengths to bear to aid tackling an area of difficulty. Nonetheless, in general, the first principle stated here in paragraph 2.16 is sound. Early identification should be built into the system.

The second point is more contentious. Is it really the case that the earlier action is taken, the less intrusive intervention will be? Surely this will depend on the needs of the child. If these include regular physiotherapy for example, will early identification reduce the disruption which might follow from the decision to carry out therapy during a school day? It is probably the case that infant or nursery classes are more flexible, certainly more so than in secondary schools, but that is a different matter.

Despite these caveats, we fully support the intention of the Code of Practice that *early* identification of SEN should be one of the aims of the identification and assessment system. Baseline assessment of children coming into school at about five years of age can, and should, be integrated into this procedure. While it is the case that the early identification of SEN is only one purpose of baseline assessment (see Chapter 4), it is a key purpose. The issue, then, is how to integrate baseline assessment into the approach advocated in the Code of Practice or another process devised by the school having had regard for the Code?

The Code itself advocates a five-stage model of identification and assessment. This built upon ideas promoted in the Warnock Report (DES 1978) and experience built up in the implementation of the 1981 Education Act. The five-stage model also is *not* mandatory. Indeed, in paragraph 2.22 it is stated that schools and LEAs might adopt different models, for example a four-stage approach. The requirement, it is argued, is that each stage shall be differentiated, and 'should aim to match action taken on behalf of a child to his or her needs'. On the basis of experience over the past few years, many schools and LEAs are considering combining stages 1 and 2, which are the responsibility of the schools, and which differ in the Code by virtue of the amount of input by the Special Needs Coordinator (SENCO) (see below).

The second point to make is that the five-stage model is not intended to be a conveyor belt, with children being placed on at stage 1 and moving inexorably to stage 5, and the award of a statement of special educational needs. The Code is explicit on this, and the thinking underlying this, and the 1993 and the earlier 1981 Education Acts, was also clear. 'Special educational needs' is a broad concept. While some children may have severe and complex difficulties, a much higher proportion have difficulties of a lesser, and/or transitory nature at some stage during their school careers. The percentages which came to be almost reified following Warnock were two and 18 per cent respectively. Hence, if about two per cent of children in an average LEA should proceed to stage 5 (the 'two per cent') and receive a statement most of the children who earlier were at stage 1 (the '18 per cent') should stay there, with increasingly small proportions moving on to subsequent stages.

In practice it has been found that these percentages are not 'givens'. This is not surprising as they did not represent objective reality in the first place, being derived from a combination of data on existing special schools and provision, and evidence from epidemiological studies of prevalence rates. Prevalence rates vary across LEAs and schools, which include different populations. Also, while the most severe disabilities lead to children unquestionably having special educational needs, this is not the case for all of the '18 per cent'. In this case, the contribution of school and parents in particular may be the key elements. For example, the high percentage of low levels of literacy found among some children might lead to their being considered to have special educational needs. Certainly a child entering secondary school with reading and spelling ages of less than seven years, say, will have significant problems accessing and responding successfully to the curriculum. If early intervention programmes ensured successful literacy development at an early age, such special needs might be prevented for some, even many of these children. We review this issue in Chapter 8.

Consequently, in the following discussion, it is important to acknowledge that the process is attempting to identify children's difficulties and their consequent needs, *not* simply to categorise and label.

School-based stages

The five-stage model includes two levels of action. The initial stages are the responsibility of the school, with stages 1 and 2 being undertaken by teachers with support from the SENCO. At stage 3, the school takes responsibility for calling in outside professionals. Stage 4 is the responsibility of the LEA, and comprises the statutory assessment, leading to Stage 5 when, and if, the LEA decides it should make a statement of special education needs. The five stages will now be discussed in more detail.

Stage 1

is characterised by the gathering of information and increased differentiation within the child's normal classroom work. (para. 2.65)

This is the stage at which *identification* first takes place. It is the point when a teacher determines that a child's development does not match the normal range of curriculum and activity or the child has a disability which should be investigated further to explore its implications.

This is an important stage. It is here that the school determines that a child is not in the normally developing category, yet does not have the depth of understanding which will follow from a thorough assessment. If children are not identified, however, such assessment will not take place. This has been the concern in the past of parents of children with specific learning difficulties/dyslexia. More recently concern has increased about autistic spectrum difficulties and Asperger's Syndrome, as well as Attention Deficit with Hyperactivity Disorder (ADHD), and children with specific speech and language difficulties (SSLD). These are all areas where children's difficulties have not always been appreciated in the past, or they have been assumed to have other problems, for example general intellectual impairment or behavioural problems arising from dysfunctional families.

At stage 1 the responsibility is on the class teacher who will identify that a child appears to have SEN. The Code of Practice recommends that the class teacher:

- identifies a child's special educational needs;
- consults the child's parents and the child;
- informs the SEN coordinator, who regulates the child's special educational needs;
- collects relevant information about the child, consulting the SEN coordinator;
- works closely with the child in the normal classroom context;
- monitors and reviews the child's progress.

Reception teachers will have relatively little information prior to the child's entry to their classes. They are likely to have some information from the parents, and pre-school experience if there was any, but the first term will be a key time in identification. Baseline assessment, *if it is designed for this purpose*, has an important contribution to make here. A well constructed process will contribute to the identification of SEN, and form the basis from which the child's progress might be monitored. The

SCAA requirement that baseline assessment shall take place after children have been in school about seven weeks is sound. By that time a teacher will have had the opportunity to gather a good deal of information, the child in the majority of cases will have settled in, and the teacher can make a reasonable assessment of the child's levels of development across different domains, rates of progress and the match with expectations.

Hence, baseline assessment should ideally be integrated into each school's SEN policy with respect to a staged model of identification and assessment. This requires that the baseline assessment contributes to a broad view of the child. A single numerical result which suggests a child has a significant delay, has some usefulness but this is limited. Is the child delayed across all domains? Is there evidence of differential development? Is there a discrepancy between, say, cognitive ability and basic skills, compared with emotional and behavioural development? To address these questions, the baseline assessment will need to cover different domains and with sufficient reliability and validity to be of use to the teacher.

At stage 1, a child's special educational needs will be registered. In practice, this has meant that a register of children has been drawn up in schools, listing children thought to have SEN. In some schools, this number reaches very high numbers with over half the number on roll being on the SEN register. The guidance from the Code is that the purpose of this registration is to note the special educational needs of individual children, in order to ensure that further investigations are undertaken, and that appropriate intervention occurs. Some LEAs now undertake an audit of children on the register, and use this percentage to allocate finance as part of the formula for funding schools. In these circumstances this register takes on a different purpose. No longer does it serve only to help specific children – rather, the more children on the register, the higher the allocation of 'SEN' finance to the school.

This clearly has a potentially confounding impact. If the sole purpose were to list children, and their SEN, teachers would consider whether a threshold degree of difficulty had been reached before undertaking registration. There is no absolute standard to determine whether a child has SEN, as we have argued above. Particularly at school entry, where a wide range of development is normal, it might be expected that teachers would be hesitant to register children unless they were reasonably sure that any difficulties or deviations from expectation were significant.

When a higher number leads to more cash, however, the bias might be in the other direction. There is clearly a 'benefit' in having a high number of children on the SEN register. Also, as we have shown in Chapter 4, if value-added analyses makes use of the proportion of children with SEN, as defined by the register, there is an additional reason to veer on the side of inclusion rather than exclusion. If children with relatively minor problems are included, they still count as a single unit, and hence a school may appear at the end of Key Stage 1 to have added considerable value. Such an 'improvement' is, of course, spurious and arises from the decision whether or not to include such children.

Hence, the inclusion of children on the SEN register is not a straightforward matter. The benefits of the register, promoted by the Code, are clear and easily defensible: beginning a systematic appraisal and education of children who might require extra, specialised, or simply different attention. But, as we have shown, the SEN register has another purpose which will confound the good intentions set out in the Code.

Evidence from two recent studies of the implementation of the Code reinforces our concerns. Derrington *et al.* (1996) investigated five LEAs which were identified as 'examples of interesting or innovative practice' (p.4). Two primary and two secondary schools were selected by LEA officers in each of the case study authorities as examples of effective practice in implementing the Code of Practice. In these 20 schools, the register of SEN was seen as the basis for a sound record-keeping system. However, Derrington *et al.* report that motivation to have a well established procedure was the fact that this was, or was becoming, one of the means of funding children with SEN. One SENCO was quoted as observing that schools had become very 'stage mindful'. Not all schools were seeking money, apparently, as another proclaimed 'with an element of pride' that their LEA adviser had noted they were under-reporting children, and so 'the school had successfully demonstrated that it was not trying to cheat the system' (p.11).

The great variation in schools' responses to the production of a register is shown in the report by Her Majesty's Inspectors following visits to 74 schools in 19 LEAs between January 1996 and March 1997 (OHMCI 1997). They present data on six schools to demonstrate this disparity.

One primary school had 39 per cent of its 367 pupils on the SEN register. Two schools from the same LEA of the same size and described as 'geographically not many miles apart' had rather different profiles for their register as Table 7.1 shows.

The following observation is made in paragraph 35.

Pupils are placed at Stages 1 and 2 on the bases of the school's own interpretation of the Code of Practice. This leads to quite marked variations from school to school, and sometimes from class to class. (OHMCI 1997, para. 35)

Table 7.1 Numbers of children on SEN register in two primary schools of similar size and location

	School A	School B
Stage 1	67	38
Stage 2	24	7
Stage 3	5	3
Stage 4	1	2
Stage 5	8	8

(from OHCMI 1997)

Stage 2

is characterised by the production of an individual education plan. (para. 2.66)

On the basis of the identification undertaken at stage 1, the class teacher will, or should, have differentiated the curriculum to attempt to meet the needs of children identified as appearing to require education different from that which would normally be provided. In some cases, modifications might be slight or easily instituted. For example, the teacher might discover the child has a mild hearing loss and so takes action to optimise the likelihood that the child hears and understands what is said. This might require doing more than sitting the child near the front – a common approach, but ineffective when, as is usual, the teacher moves around and addresses the class from different points in the room.

For other children, a more systematic, sustained and changing approach may be necessary. For example:

Natalie entered school with impaired speech. She had been receiving speech therapy for about a year, although this had not been intensive. Her mother reported that therapy was helping her, but she was still difficult to understand. Over the first few weeks her teacher noted that she spoke very little and appeared to have a limited understanding of the vocabulary and instructions she would normally expect. After about five weeks her teacher completed the Infant Index on Natalie. This revealed that her behaviour, including her concentration, was satisfactory, but that her language and early learning skills were poorly developed. The scale identified she was at the 1st centile on the Basic Skills Subscale.

On the basis of this combination of instructional observations together with the results of a standardised observation schedule, Infant Index, Natalie was placed at stage 1. In this case Natalie's development in this important domain was found to be delayed by using a scale which had been developed and standardised. This supplemented evidence from the teacher's own observations. Placing Natalie on the SEN register was reasonable, given this evidence and the need to be alert to the need to modify the curriculum.

Returning to Natalie, identified at stage 1:

Natalie's progress was reviewed over the next half term, including discussions with her mother. At this point it was agreed that a more systematic approach to her language needs was required, to supplement that available as part of the teacher's usual approach to Reception children. Consequently, an Individual Education Plan (IEP) was devised. This focused on language, but was related to the ongoing general work in class. At this point the IEP contained targets for vocabulary and the understanding of a number of syntactic structures. A variety of tasks were used, both with peers who had normal language development, and supplemented by work at home. Natalie's teacher was keen, at this age, that the 'work' should be fun and comparable to the normal activities of the class. Natalie's programme was reviewed by her teacher each two weeks, when new targets and tasks were set. She was reviewed with her parents after another term, and again at the end of the Summer term.

Note. Natalie's needs have been addressed by an individual programme; this is sequential, with targets and tasks built upon each other; and review and reappraisal are built in. On the other hand, the teacher has not had the benefit of outside specialists. This was deliberate as the evidence suggested that there were activities which could reasonably be undertaken, and that she was successful in this approach.

The drawing up and implementation of the IEP is one of the major characteristics of stage 2. The purpose is to help the child, but the HMI review of the Code (OHMCI 1997) has demonstrated that again, practice varies and confusion exists:

Schools are worried or confused over the way in which IEPs are used by inspectors and officers for the purposes of accountability. There is sometimes a feeling that they need to be published documents to withstand legal scrutiny rather than a practical basis for individualised planning. These worries have led some SENCOs to lose sight of the purpose of individual education plans. IEPs are successful where they promote effective planning by teachers and assist pupils to make progress through the setting and reviewing of practical learning targets. (para. 77)

Another manifestation of accountability is the OFSTED inspection. Her Majesty's Inspectors note that concern about these can lead to inappropriate responses, including one newly appointed SENCO attempting to produce 174 IEPs in one term in order to show the forthcoming OFSTED inspection team that IEPs were available. As HMI note, 'this became a paper exercise devoid of any links with teachers, parents or pupils' (OHMCI 1997, para. 78). Once again we see that the sound educational rationale underlying the development of intervention is confounded with the alternative agenda of accountability.

Stage 3

According to the Code of Practice, stage 3 is the point at which outside specialist support is called in. This will follow the implementation of the IEP, a review of the success of the programme and a decision that further investigation and/or advice is necessary. This may follow a series of implementation–review cycles at stage 2. Indeed, the majority of children at stage 2 are expected to stay at that level. But in a minority of cases, further exploration is required.

Once again, the SENCO, in collaboration with parents and teacher(s), will take the lead. Assuming that the baseline assessment was helpful and led to intervention at stages 1 and 2, there should be a coherent pathway leading to stage 3.

Lee was assessed using Baseline-*plus* and found to have difficulties in the domains of language and concentration. Also, he was rather shy and not very forthcoming. His teacher developed modifications to her programmes to address these characteristics, but with only limited success. At stage 2, the SENCO and teacher developed an IEP aimed to address his language needs, which were considered to reflect a limited early experience. He responded a little, but continued not to engage in much class activity and not to make progress in basic subjects.

The SENCO sought advice from the visiting educational psychologist. Having discussed ideas informally, observed Lee in class and carried out individual work outside the classroom, the psychologist reported that Lee had strengths which had not been fully appreciated. Although his language usage was limited he had demonstrated an above average knowledge of vocabulary when he did not have to speak. Also, in a range of other non-verbal tasks, Lee performed at a level which was average or better for his age.

In this case the school had followed a sound approach but the expertise of the psychologist revealed facets of the child's development previously unseen in class. In this instance the psychologist not only worked with Lee in class, alongside the teacher, but also in a different part of the school. In-class work is often very useful, and collaborative assessment by the teacher and specialist can be very rewarding. In some cases, however, the information acquired from a different route may be crucial. In this instance, Lee showed a very different side of his development. This can be irritating to teachers who feel that as a child is in a one-to-one situation, they can achieve their best, can't they? The point is however, not to be critical of teachers for not producing the same data, but to explore the effect of task, setting and presentation, and of their interactions. In the case of Lee, both setting and task were crucial in revealing new information.

On the basis of this, the teacher and psychologist drafted a new programme which played to Lee's non-verbal strengths. They discussed this with his mother who was willing to collaborate on a programme of support at home which integrated with that provided by the teachers.

In Lee's case, only the educational psychologist contributed and the resultant programme, monitored and adapted over the next year, worked well. Lee gained self-confidence and using his greater opportunities with non-verbal tasks he improved his motivation. These factors, together with a straightforward but structured approach to literacy, helped Lee to make a good start with his reading and spelling. In other cases, the first outside specialist might be a SEN support teacher from the LEA; an education welfare officer, if attendance or home factors appear important contributions; or a professional from the health service, a speech and language therapist for example.

Determining the correct specialist, and a sequence if necessary, is not always straightforward. When there is a well established and available SEN support teacher team, this will often be the first port of call for educational reasons. The HMI survey found that while these services for children with sensory impairment were seen by schools as 'easily accessible and suitably specific' (paragraph 92), the learning support services and those for children with behavioural problems were more problematic. Many learning support services have been subject to reorganisation and redeployment, often implemented at very short notice (paragraph 93), and in over a quarter of the LEAs there has been a reduction in staffing levels. HMI report that because of the lack of a service or its minimal quantity, in some LEAs stage 3 of the Code does not really exist.

A similar concern was expressed about speech and language therapy services. HMI report that schools were often 'extremely dissatisfied with the limited help they receive from services for pupils with speech and language difficulties' (paragraph 104). On the other hand, support from educational psychologists was seen by primary school SENCOs as valuable. Educational psychologists' time was constrained by the number of statutory assessments at stage 4, but their availability for involvement at earlier stages was found to be useful. In some cases educational psychologists will contribute to the support of children at stages 1 and 2 by discussing issues in general or contributing to the teachers' awareness through formal or informal in-service training.

While stage 3 is characterised by bringing in specialists from outside the school to aid assessment and intervention, it is not the case that *no* such action should take place prior to then. Parents need to give permission, *informed* consent, before such a professional works with their child, but there are wider and consultative contributions that specialists can make. Once more the SENCO is the key professional, weighing up the school's needs to ensure optimal delivery of the scarce support services. The picture coming through from surveys of practice is one where many schools attempt to follow the Code too rigidly or mechanically, while more successful practice is associated with adherence to the con-ceptualisation and principles: having regard to the Code.

Stages 4 and 5: outside professionals

Stage 4

Following specialist analysis and advice intervention will be directed to the achievement of various targets, and the child will be reviewed. In most cases it is accepted that the child either remains at stage 3 or returns to a lower stage, but in a minority of cases a child may move to stage 4. At this point the LEA agrees to undertake an assessment when it is probable that a statement of special educational needs is necessary. Note that stage 4 is a period of *assessment*. Many have incorrectly termed this process 'statementing'. It is not, for although the process starts when there is a probability of a statement, it is fundamentally an assessment and an outcome may be that no statement is required. We are not being merely pedantic in our insistence that professionals and parents do not refer to this process as 'statementing'.

It is at this point that the success or otherwise of the previous procedures can be clearly seen. Where baseline assessment was valid or useful and this linked into a process of assessment, planning, implementation and review, the child's movement through to stage 4 should not only be coherent, it should ensure that at this point there is a wealth of useful information. For example, details of attempts to assess the child's difficulties and the child's needs will be clear. The relative benefits of different approaches, and types and quantity of provision can be judged. Also the assessment and advice from outside specialists at stage 3 will be available. In the best cases, therefore, the LEA should have no difficulty in determining *whether* to undertake a stage 4 assessment. Furthermore, much of the required information will be available. It is not necessary, for example, that the information needed to produce the advice is all collected after the LEA's decision to undertake assessment. Indeed, the LEA may decide not to seek particular advice if it has obtained such advice within the previous 12 months and the parent, professional providing the advice and the LEA itself are all content that this is sufficient for the purpose of arriving at a satisfactory assessment. [(Regulation 6(5) of the Statutory Instrument No. 1047, 1994].

Stage 5

Stage 5 is the process whereby the LEA draws up a statement. A well developed system should allow a speedy response to the LEA's call for advice and as a result the LEA should be able quickly to determine whether a statement should be written, and the content. The length of time taken in the past has been the subject of considerable criticism (e.g. the Audit Commission and Her Majesty's Inspectors (1992). It is worrying to find that HMI in their most recent report (OHMCI 1997) still express dissatisfaction with the time taken and indeed with the arbitrariness of the LEAs' decisions. Also the Audit Commission (1995) provided data on the performance of all LEAs with respect to achieving the time targets for the production of a draft statement. The variation in the percentages achieved by different LEAs is remarkable. Interestingly there does not appear to be a direct relationship between the performance and the number of appeals to the SEN Tribunal. Table 7.2 provides a selection of LEAs to demonstrate both range and this lack of relationship.

Table 7.2 Comparison of the performance of six LEAs

LEA	% statements in 6 months	Number of appeals[1]
Barnet	>80	5.1
Dudley	>80	2.67
Cheshire	>80	2.45
Walsall	1	1.03
Enfield	0	1.66
Ealing	0	5.31

[1]Number of appeals per 10,000 of the school population

Source:
Annual Report of the SEN Tribunal 1994–5
Audit Commission: *Local Authority Performance Indicators 1994–5*

There are two main issues here. The first concerns overall level of resourcing to allow the jobs to be carried out and carried out effectively. Interestingly, the Audit Commission considered that the time variations reported above were not relative to staff levels. The second factor concerns the effectiveness of the system as a whole. As we have agreed, this needs to be coherent, logical and flexible. It needs to have the task of clarifying and providing for children's needs as its first priority.

Conclusion

The Code of Practice has generally been welcomed and reports such as that of Her Majesty's Inspectors (OHMCI 1997) reveal that it has made a significant impact. Baseline assessment is a key element and it is essential that each school incorporates this into its SEN procedures. The Code has raised the profile of SEN and the role of the SENCO. Great stress has been put on this new professional – remember this role did not exist as such until the 1993 Education Act and the Code of Practice. The need to have a SENCO has had a positive impact throughout the school system.

Inevitably practice is patchy in this early period, but improving. Clearly it is to be hoped that all practice reaches appropriate levels of quality very quickly. Records are very important but they are not the whole story. There is a need for a basic level of resourcing to enable identification and assessment, let alone special provision to be made. The cuts reported by HMI indicate that this does not obtain in some LEAs. In addition, however, there is a need to ensure the system is appropriate as a system. In the primary school this requires that children are appraised over their first few weeks in Reception. This should build upon information from any pre-school provision and that provided by the parents.

We fully support the use of school early baseline assessment at a suitable point, after about half a term, permitting a period to allow a settling in and a broad general sensitisation of the teacher to the characteristics of the children and the class (Lindsay 1981). Consequently, we support the requirements set down with respect to timing by SCAA (1997d). But time is only one consideration. Of greater importance is the *acceptance* of the baseline assessment procedure.

The Infant Index (Desforges and Lindsay 1995a) predecessor to Baseline-*plus*, was developed as a means of initial identification of SEN and as an approach which could link in with the Code of Practice stage 1. Not all baseline assessment procedures had this intention. In our opinion however this is a crucial purpose and the need for integration between the baseline assessment and SEN procedures is essential. If this is not the case, where perhaps the baseline assessment provides a minimum amount of information, schools will run two procedures, which will be costly and inefficient. Interestingly, despite valuable views on a range of matters, the recent HMI review of the implementation of the Code of Practice (OHMCI 1997) does not refer to baseline assessment in its comments on identification of pupils with SEN. While no statutory requirement for baseline assessment existed at that time, many LEAs and schools had such a procedure in place.

Looking to the future, we hope to see a full and functional integration of baseline assessment into schools' SEN procedures and general curriculum planning. The Code of Practice provides a sound framework of guidance which, if followed flexibly, forms a welcome support to effective practice. For this to occur, it is necessary to keep always at the front of our thinking the fact that the purpose of the Code is to help individual children. The use of baseline assessment for value-added analysis, and the percentage of children at various stages for audit purposes, are separate functions. At worst, these can become distractions or even impediments. The task, therefore, is to maintain the focus on optimising the education of children.

Chapter 8

Interventions

The purpose of baseline assessment is two-fold. Firstly, the information collected on the children at school entry allows teachers to take action in the short term. Secondly, the collection of information over time allows a longer-term review of practice, leading to possible changes. Returning to our typology of the purposes set out in Chapter 1, we may see that the child-based purposes are essentially linked with short- and medium-term initiatives, as set out in our model in Chapter 3. Here, the teacher will take note of the information from the baseline assessment as a screen and provider of data on current performance. This might be followed up by a further screen, and/or a more detailed assessment of children considered to have difficulties. Also, for those children who are judged to be progressing satisfactorily, to have 'passed' the baseline assessment, the information adds to that available to the teacher from other sources for use in gaining a picture of the class for the purpose of general curriculum planning.

The school-based purposes, on the other hand, are mainly medium to long term. Leaving aside the issue of determination of the SEN element of the school budget formula, both school accountability and school improvement are activities which require action over years rather than days. However, in both cases intervention is the outcome of the baseline assessment, and in each case the aim is to make improvements to the educational opportunities of children.

Intervention for children with educational difficulties

Baseline assessment enables teachers to identify children who are having difficulties. As we argued in Chapter 1, these might be of two kinds, representing different conceptualisations.

Low attainment

Baseline assessment allows the teacher to identify children whose attainment is at a relatively low level, whether measured against a norm (e.g. in the bottom 15 per cent) or a standard (e.g. unable to read ten words). A similar approach might be made to questions of behaviour and social development.

Diagnostic

A second approach distinguishes the *nature* and *cause* of the child's difficulties. These might be related to a variety of factors, including:

- constitutional – e.g. gender, birth injury, viral infection
- environmental – limited educational opportunities, family stress, fear (e.g. of racism)
- instructional – inadequate or inappropriate curriculum content, materials and teaching method.

The nature of the difficulty might be considered as an impairment in one or more of the following domains:

- cognitive – general delay in cognitive ability; specific difficulty, e.g. phonological processing
- sensory – e.g. hearing impairment, and its degree; general hearing loss versus high frequency loss
- social-emotional – e.g. emotionally labile; unhappy, withdrawn
- behavioural – e.g. impulsive; attention control difficulties; high activity levels; aggressive.

The former approach focuses on the behaviour itself, for example the level of reading of a seven year old, while the latter, the diagnostic, attempts to offer explanations. Each could lead to different types of intervention, but the basis would be different. In the case of the 'low attainment' approach, there might be different degrees or types of input on the basis of the extent to which children differed from the expected level. Hence, there might be intervention for the lowest five per cent, which might be very intensive, while for the next ten per cent the intervention would be less frequent. In the latter case, however, intervention would be designed to match the hypothesised cause. Consequently, children thought to have severe emotional difficulties might receive a form of therapeutic approach, e.g. play therapy-based, to enable them to work through trauma and become able to learn effectively. A child considered to have phonological coding difficulties might be given intensive practice in this domain while children with experiential limitations might receive help designed initially to increase their understanding of the world, of language, to develop vocabulary and the meaning of print.

Hence, the interventions which might follow from baseline assessment might be driven and shaped by very different conceptualisations. For the purpose of the present discussion we shall focus on literacy, but the arguments will generalise to other educational areas.

National Literacy Strategy

The National Literacy Strategy (Literacy Task Force 1997) is firmly in the former mould, although there is some reference to the latter. The approach is to set targets:

- 80 per cent of all 11 year olds will reach the standards expected of their age in English (i.e. Level 4) in the Key Stage 2 National Curriculum tests.

The Secretary of State is quoted as having requested a strategy which will ensure that:

By the end of the second term of a Labour government, all children leaving primary school . . . will have reached a reading age of at least eleven. (p.13)

However, despite this all-encouraging target there is a caveat:

Our goal is that ultimately almost all children will achieve this target, although we recognise that a small number of children might not be able to do so because of their special educational needs. (p.13)

Thus, it is assumed by the Task Force that the target is not realisable by all, but the explanation is that it is the 'special educational needs' which prevent this. This is, inherently, a curious notion: a child's SEN might be that he or she requires particular support *in order to* achieve this target, rather than be used as an explanation why this is not possible.

The strategy adopted has two elements. The first is systemic, e.g. the development of nursery education, changes to initial teacher training to increase emphasis on literacy, and extending continuing professional development of teachers, again with an emphasis on literacy. The National Literacy Project also recommends responsibilities for the management of schools and the government's role. Literacy consultants have been employed and detailed proposals are set out for the training courses and consultancy which is envisaged.

The requirements for schools to teach the National Curriculum were criticised, and the Task Force advocated a higher priority for literacy and numeracy. This has been supported by the Secretary of State, David Blunkett, and consultation on modifying requirements is continuing, but already OFSTED have issued advice to inspectors that schools are not to be expected necessarily to follow the programmes of study in the six non-core subjects.

National Curriculum assessments are considered important, if they test literacy effectively, are consistent over time, provide detailed information on literacy performance and ensure public credibility. Baseline assessment is mentioned specifically:

> The achievement of our objectives will be served by the introduction of baseline assessment for five year olds entering school and by the continuing refinement of Key Stage 1 tests in English. These will enable schools to set individual targets for progress and enable early intervention where problems are identified. This is particularly important in relation to children who have, or might develop, learning difficulties. Also, primary schools will have comparative, value-added and improvement information on which to base targets and other management decisions. (para. 63, p.28)

With respect to children with SEN, the report has four paragraphs. Literacy needs should be covered as part of individual education plans (IEPs) and baseline assessment should be used to identify children with SEN and linked to the Code of Practice stages of identification and assessment. Parent involvement, including family literacy, is promoted.

In addition to these initiatives, the Task Force recommends action, for children generally, with respect to parental responsibilities, family literacy and initiatives such as summer literacy schools. This is, therefore, a strategy which has major implications across the education system.

The second element focuses on the teaching of literacy itself. Drawing upon 'Ofsted and other research' (p.15), a description of the successful teaching of reading is given:

The successful teaching of reading in particular:

- equips pupils at the earliest stage to draw on the sources of knowledge needed when reading for meaning, including phonic knowledge (simple and complex sound/symbol relationships), graphic knowledge (patterns within words), word recognition (a sight vocabulary which includes common features of words), grammatical knowledge (checking for sense through the ways words are organised) and contextual information (meaning derived from the text as a whole);

- continues the direct teaching of reading techniques through both key stages, building systematically on the skills pupils have learnt earlier in, for example, tackling unfamiliar words;
- provides a range of reading material, usually based around a core reading programme, but substantially enriched with other good quality material, including information tests;
- stimulates and requires good library use;
- extends pupils' reading by focused work on challenging texts with the whole class or in groups;
- involves frequent opportunities for pupils to hear, read and discuss texts and to think about the content and the language used; and
- gives time for productive individual reading at school and at home, and opportunities for pupils to share their response with others.

(Literacy Task Force, pp.15–16)

Again, this approach is for children across the board. The 'literacy hour', for example, is for all children, albeit that for some of the time children might be in groups, and presumably such groups might be determined by level of attainment. The literacy hour is set out in Table 8.1

The National Literacy Strategy, and the National Literacy Project (NLP) which comprises the detailed elements for intervention, present a remarkable change in the approach to literacy in this country. Previously, matters of intervention would be left to the individual professional judgements of teachers, or their group decisions. However, their judgements, and the practice which follows, was clearly influenced both by their initial training and the guidance of the LEA, which could be a light touch or more direct. As baseline assessment develops, the system of intervention must be heavily weighted towards that prescribed by the government. The literacy hour for example, might not be mandatory, in that there might be no statutory basis, but what position will OFSTED adopt? Will schools decide on alternative methods in the face of such centralised pressure?

This issue strikes at the heart of professionalism, but too much can be made of that. For example, we expect other professionals to adopt best practices and do not expect widely differing approaches if we have an operation, visit a lawyer, or consult a surveyor. We assume there might be some debate about optimal procedures when an operation, for example, is new but then an orthodoxy will be agreed to which surgeons subscribe. Careful research of new approaches might lead to a challenge, to a revision of that orthodoxy. On the other hand, where evidence is not clear, or where there is no known effective intervention (e.g. the common cold, or the many viruses which affect hundreds of thousands each year but which have no cure) practice might vary.

Table 8.1 The literacy hour

	Key Stage 1	Key Stage 2
Whole class (approx. 15 minutes)	Shared text work (a balance of reading and writing)	Shared text work (a balance of reading and writing)
Whole class (approx. 15 minutes)	Focused word work	A balance over the term of focused word work or sentence work
Group work (approx. 20 minutes)	1. Independent reading, writing or word work activities 2. Teacher works with each group twice in the week, focused on guided reading	1. Independent reading, writing word and sentence activities 2. Teacher works with each group for a sustained period (15 minutes) each week on guided reading or writing
Whole class (approx. 10 minutes)	Reviewing, reflecting upon and presenting work covered in the lesson	Reviewing, reflecting upon and presenting work covered in the lesson

Fundamentally, therefore, the reason either for orthodoxy and conformity, or experimentation, should be based on evidence. Medicine has taken this on board and is developing a strategy which is 'evidence based'. The National Literacy Programmes and Strategy claim to be evidence based. As shown above, the Task Force assert that 'both OFSTED and other research' suggest that the successful teaching of literacy should 'in general' comprise the elements listed (p.15). The question arises, therefore, whether evidence does support this prescription? In one sense, the answer is undoubtedly in the affirmative, as the statements are general and comprehensive. There is little that has not been included, although exceptions concern children's *oral language ability*, the *priorities* to be accorded within the list, and the *psychological principles* which research has indicated as relevant to learning.

Language ability

Work currently being undertaken by one of us has indicated the strong relationship between literacy and language in children with specific speech and language difficulties (Dockrell and Lindsay 1998). The literacy levels of a sample of 69 children with SSLD were found to be 2:3 years behind chronological age for reading accuracy, 2:4 years behind for reading comprehension (both measured by the Macmillan Individual Reading Analysis) and 1:8 years behind for spelling (British Ability Scales II) – see Dockrell and Lindsay (1997).

Priorities

The NLP implies importance in as much as detailed lists of elements must be covered. The literacy hour has designated times, to the minute, for activities, and Annex A sets out lists of competencies. There are three strands:

word level	phonics, spelling or vocabulary
sentence level	grammar and punctuation
text level	comprehension and composition

Each has its place during the hour. What is not clear, however, is the variation from these implicit priorities that might be appropriate for different children. The force of the document is to argue that the priorities will be identical for all, and indeed the two allocations will be identical. There is no help to be found in the section on children with SEN (pp.31–2). Is it the case that all children with severe reading difficulties will benefit from this carefully designated literacy hour? The scope for variation is limited. Forty minutes are for whole class activities, with only 20 minutes for group work. Also, within the group work at Key Stage 1, the focus of teacher involvement is to be guided reading, plus individual reading, writing or word work activities.

Psychological principles

The NLP makes no explicit mention of psychological principles which concern children's learning. Some are implicit, including the importance of motivation and the importance of identifying prior knowledge and difficulties. However, these are presented as strategies for successful *teaching* rather than *learning*. Indeed, this neglect of learning at the expense of teaching can be found in other initiatives, most strikingly in the new standards for initial teacher training (Teacher Training Agency 1997). In addition, it appears that the literacy hour is based upon an assumption of what low attainers require. Is this, even if true, appropriate for children developing normally, or at an advanced rate? Furthermore, is it wise that government should determine pedagogy?

In this section we shall consider just two principles. The first is that of massed versus distributed practice, and will be exemplified below in our discussion of the Essex Reading Research Project. The NLP *requires* that there be a literacy hour – 'All classes must teach literacy for one hour, per day of continuous, dedicated time' (p.48).

It is stated that there is 'scope for some adjustment to meet the needs of particular classes' but this appears to be for the early stages of the project. Given that this is to cover both Key Stages 1 and 2, there is no recognition that such a period of time might not be appropriate for both five- and 11-year-olds. Also, this approach masses practice during a day, although by having sessions each day there is some distribution. The Essex project, on the other hand, has several sessions per day, of a shorter interval.

The second factor is that of sequence. There appears to be an assumption that there is a particular sequence by which knowledge and skills might be acquired. This is generally not unreasonable, if only because most children are exposed to sequences determined by teachers or parents already. On the other hand, different sequences might either be as effective, or in the case of certain children be optimal. For example, it is common to teach the vowels before vowel digraphs (e.g. 'ee', 'oo'). In our experience of working with children with a variety of learning difficulties, such set down sequences based on logic and adult educationists' judgements can only be a guide. Some children will learn sound–letter combinations in a different order. The point concerns true individual-isation of learning, rather than individualisation by teaching.

Carefully structured approaches to teaching and learning assume that learning occurs in fixed, sequential hierarchies that are followed by the majority of children. Although many theories of child development use stage models to describe the acquisition of new skills or competencies,

125

there are alternatives. Donaldson (1978) has developed a model of children's learning where interests, motivation, context, and prior experiences are attributed an important role in influencing which cognitive strategies are used in problem-solving situations. Learning is seen as a network rather than a predetermined sequential activity, with the child making connections between previously isolated areas of knowledge and skills, and moving continuously from the known to the unknown by routes that are often difficult to predict.

If we impose the same structured approach on all children it is likely that some will benefit and have their learning enhanced, but it is also possible that some children will have their learning impaired. At issue here, conceptually, is the *level* of specificity or generalisation of a process. For example, it is reasonable to conclude from research that children generally benefit from 'structured' approaches, but the detail of such structures when turned into a programme may need to be differentiated from one child to the next, to take account of both cognitive factors and the range of other influences such as those described above.

This leads to one of the criticisms of the reliance on diagnostic categories, for example dyslexic, autistic or having ADHD: the child concerned is an individual and will require a programme suited to his or her needs. This is not to argue against particular approaches, whether they be multi-sensory teaching, special diets or the literacy hour. The point is to acknowledge that, even where appropriate, any particular approach has a *range of application* and will not be appropriate in all cases, or more probably will be appropriate to varying degrees. Hence there is an issue of the degree of applicability of a principle, in addition to the evidence for the importance of the principle itself.

Other evidence from research

We have examined the National Literacy Strategy and National Literacy Project in some detail as these will clearly set the context and main approach to literacy development for the foreseeable future. But what of other research? Does the NLP truly reflect the research evidence? In this section we shall discuss briefly recent and current research projects, and also review meta-analyses which have provided perspectives on successful teaching and learning. We shall focus, again, on literacy and examine a small number of key themes.

Are all poor readers the same?

Implicit in the NLP is a common approach, with some degree of individualisation. However, as we discussed at the start of this chapter, a different orientation is to start from the premise that children will learn differently, and hence require different teaching, depending upon the nature of learning strategies. Learning might be idiosyncratic.

Evidence on children with literacy difficulties provides useful guidance. There has been a long and at times acrimonious debate about the 'existence' of dyslexia, or specific learning difficulties (SpLD). Discussed by some as a middle-class phenomenon, research has built up on both the nature of the children's difficulties and on the political implications (e.g. Pumfrey and Reason 1991). Recently, the focus has changed. There is now common agreement that some children do have significantly impaired reading development, and that this cuts across social class. Indeed, studies using children attending the independent Dyslexia Institute show sizeable numbers of working-class children (Riddick 1996).

Two major issues arise: is there a difference between children designated dyslexic and other children with low attainment, and do these two groups require different forms of intervention? Researchers such as Stanovich (1994, 1998) and Siegel (1992) have argued that there is no compelling evidence that dyslexic children differ from others with poor literacy. In other words, there is a continuum, rather than a dichotomy, and each group may be considered to have a 'reading disability' Leaving aside those children who have a quite separate likely cause (e.g. long-term school absence, severe emotional difficulties, hearing impairments), the major factor for these children with a reading disability, they argue, is a deficiency in phonological processing. This includes awareness of sound and rhyme, ability to segment words into phonemes, and fluency with sounds.

The evidence is now very strong that phonological processing is a major factor. However, as Nicholson (1996) argues, this does not prove that there is *no* difference between subgroups. It might be that phonological processing is the cause of reading disability, but it might equally be true, logically, that there is a more fundamental cause leading to phonological deficits. In this case, it is possible that there are, in fact, two causes, leading to the same problem in reading.

This argument has been extended by Coltheart and Jackson (1998) who argue that reading involves a set of processing subsystems and, for any individual child, a problem in one system might either be a proximal (a closer, more direct) or a distal (more removed) cause. Also, children with

127

the same proximal cause might have different distal causes. Take two children each having reading difficulties characterised by an inability to map letters to sounds. In each case this is the proximal cause. However, while for one child this is determined by poor phonological processing, for the other child the distal cause might be ineffective teaching.

Secondly, it is also the case that even if phonological deficit is the fundamental cause, other factors might mediate its impact. In our model, these factors might affect the phonological deficit itself, or operate on the child's compensatory mechanisms. Also, we have so far described causal linkages at the level of cognition. If we go to more fundamental aspects, to the biological basis of brain function, then we must consider genetic and other influences – see the Forum on Dyslexia in the Child Psychology and Psychiatry Review 1998 issue 1 for a recent review of these issues.

This second approach is essentially the argument put forward by Solity who has been carrying out an intervention study, the Essex Reading Research Project. Working with educational psychologists from Essex LEA in six experimental and six comparison schools, Solity has based an intervention programme on a theory of instruction which focuses on the action of the teacher, rather than any assumptions about the children as learners. At the end of the first year, the reception children are reported to have made very good progress in basic literacy, with mean scores of children from the experimental schools being significantly higher on all measures except rhyming (Solity 1998). Also, using the project's aggregated score across several measures of basic literacy (e.g. British Ability Scales Word Reading) there were large and significant differences in the numbers of low scores. While 49 per cent of children in the comparison schools had a score of 35 or lower, this applied to only nine per cent in the experimental schools. A similar, but opposite, discrepancy was found at the top end, with many more high achievers in the experimental schools. Finally, at the start of the next school year, only one per cent of the experimental school children were designated low achievers by the project's criteria, against 21 per cent in the comparison schools. This study is still underway, and these results must be regarded as interim, and hence with caution. However, they provide support for the view that it is the nature of teaching or instruction which is the key rather than the nature of the children's individual difficulties.

A large-scale longitudinal study in Albany, New York, provides a further perspective. Vellutino et al. (1996) carried out a project with 827 children from two cohorts in 17 schools. They selected children with low attainment in literacy, including only those who met the usual exclusion criteria (e.g. IQ greater than 90 on either the Verbal or Performance scale of the Revised Wechsler Intelligence Scale for Children). The experimental group of 188, 9 per cent of the total, received daily one-to-one tuition of 30 minutes duration over 15 weeks (typically 75–80 sessions). They received a rich and varied programme including work at the level of sounds, whole words and text from specially trained tutors. Progress was compared against that of normal readers and a contrast group of poor readers who received the usual school 'small group' extra help ('small' could be up to nine!).

The interesting point for the present discussion is that the outcomes show differential rates of progress within the group as a whole. The largest group, 67.1 per cent of the poor readers, developed to be within the average or above average range after one semester of tutoring. Overall, only 12 children or 1.5 per cent scored below the 15th centile of a composite measure of reading. Vellutino *et al.* conclude, along with Marie Clay, that:

> most impaired readers, who might be classified as learning disabled, are probably not learning disabled in the stereotypical sense in which the term is used, that is, as a label for someone whose learning difficulties are presumed to be of constitutional origin. (p.629)

However, some children, despite this intensive and generally successful intervention, made limited progress. While phonological difficulties were found to be the major area of weakness across the children in general, reinforcing the evidence quoted above (see also Hatcher *et al.* 1994), the researchers also argue that their results provide support for there being a small group of children with a significant 'deficit' of constitutional origin.

Let us return to our original question – are all poor readers the same? The evidence points at present to the following conclusions.

- There are some children whose poor reading is due to non-cognitive factors including poor attendance, prolonged ill health, sensory impairments.
- Some children have a greater difficulty in learning to read than their general cognitive ability and lack of other possible causal explanation would predict.
- Some children fail to acquire literacy as a result of inadequate teaching. This might relate to limited resources, limited or inappropriate training, literacy having a 'low priority', etc.
- Children with a 'reading disability' most commonly show a form of phonological processing deficit.
- In most children this might be overcome by intensive relatively

short-term comprehensive intervention.
- This leaves a very small percentage (probably one or two per cent) who will continue to require long-term intensive support.

Hence, the evidence reviewed has suggested that, on the whole, a large proportion of children considered to have a 'reading disability' or dyslexia have problems most particularly with phonological processing, and that intensive early support can overcome these. While not all children with literacy problems are 'the same', the evidence points to the likely success of similar, albeit intensive, teaching approaches. In this sense, there is no simple answer to the question as the sameness/difference might be examined at the level of teaching requirements, symptom, cause(s) or possible more fundamental cause(s). But these are issues mainly of interest to researchers. For the teacher, the evidence points to a programme which is basically *similar* for all children displaying limited literacy skills at the age of five to six years.

One-to-one tutoring

Our conclusion at the end of the previous section suggested that well developed programmes could improve the basic literacy attainments of the great number of children who are low attainers at school entry, and during the period five to six years of age. In this sense, the evidence is supportive of the arguments in the National Literacy Programme. However, what is played down, and indeed has no specified role in the NLP, is the place of one-to-one tutoring. This is referred to in the eighth of the ten points derived from research findings: 'uses carefully sequenced, whole class, group and individual work to focus on strategies and skills . . .' (Literacy Task Force 1997, p.15). It is not difficult to see why. Either their distillation of research did not indicate one-to-one tutoring was an important element, or else its inherent cost was considered to be prohibitive.

There is an obvious face validity to the hypothesis that the smaller the group size the better for learning, and hence the optimal being one-to-one. However, it is important to consider purpose and the empirical evidence. It should also be stated that while cost is a proper and inevitable consideration, it is separate.

One-to-one tutoring goes on in many guises probably in all schools, and there are many reports of small-scale projects. Large-scale evaluations, and meta-analyses of large numbers of studies are important for gaining a clear picture of the overall evidence. The two main approaches are tutoring by teachers (or teacher assistants), parent tutoring schemes (e.g. Paired Reading – see Topping and Lindsay 1992 for a review), and peer tutoring schemes (Topping 1988). The evidence for both peer and parent tutoring schemes is now substantial. Both are low-cost initiatives requiring a limited amount of teaching but producing significant success across large numbers of children. In addition to Paired Reading, there are simpler schemes (e.g. Relaxed Reading, Lindsay et al. 1984) and schemes which are a little more complex (e.g. Pause Prompt and Praise, Glynn et al. 1987). Peer tutoring schemes have the additional benefit of improvement in skills in the other child acting as tutor, as well as the tutee.

Success for teacher-based tutoring schemes is also substantiated. The most well known is probably Reading Recovery (Clay 1985). This is a well constructed scheme which takes children not at school entry, but after a period of normal teaching. Those children who are in the bottom group in terms of attainment at the age of six years are then given a wide ranging programme of work, using one-to-one tutoring, for 30 minutes per day. After a period of about a term those who have been raised to the average range are discontinued. The teachers are all experienced, with additional, specific training in the delivery of Reading Recovery. Evaluations in this country have shown Reading Recovery to be successful (e.g. Sylva and Hurry 1995). Also, comparisons of Reading Recovery and other programmes, e.g. Success for All, demonstrate not only the success of Reading Recovery but also the benefits of one-to-one tutoring, including its cost effectiveness (Wasik and Slavin 1993, Ross et al. 1995).

A study by Iversen and Tunmer (1993), however, suggested that the success of Reading Recovery could be enhanced by additional systematic instruction in phonological skills development. Both a standard Reading Recovery group and a 'modified' Reading Recovery group achieved significantly better scores after intervention than a control group which had received the normally available resources for at-risk readers. However, the modified Reading Recovery group reached discontinuation significantly earlier, a mean of 41.75 lessons as compared with 57.31 lessons for the standard Reading Recovery group. A study by Hatcher et al. (1994), using individual tuition, 40 lessons of 30 minutes over 20 weeks, also reported the superiority for seven-year-old poor readers of a Reading Recovery with Phonology teaching programme.

Studies such as these, and those of Wasik and Slavin and Ross et al. all indicate the benefits of one-to-one tutoring. However, these benefits are not independent of the method used. While Reading Recovery has been shown to be effective, the addition of specific instruction in aspects of phonology appears to enhance the effectiveness of the method. The results of Success for All, which also emphasises learning to read in meaningful contexts, indicates the importance of an approach which is broad-based.

Some conclusions regarding intervention

We have argued that baseline assessment has an important role in identifying children who might be at risk of failing to develop early educational skills. The evidence from a number of studies of early intervention for literacy development indicates that a focus in the early years, ages five to seven, will be beneficial.

The National Literacy Project emphasises class and group activity, and the deterrent of cost is identified as a reason why Reading Recovery has not been further supported. Support for the former position, if not for the detailed approach, comes from the early results of the Essex Reading Research Project (Solity 1998). Wasik and Slavin (1993) have reviewed the results of 16 studies using five different tutoring methods and offer a series of recommendations for programmes. Drawing upon such studies we offer the following recommendations for intervention.

1. Intervention must be based upon a sound foundation. That which is for specific children relies upon their correct identification. Further, the elements of skill and knowledge requiring differentiated intervention must also be correctly identified. Consequently, for early intervention, baseline assessment procedures must be reliable and valid, as a minimum, and also give pointers to appropriate, specific intervention.

2. The model of reading must be comprehensive, with action at the level of the word, sentence and text. Reading Recovery has sound indication of effectiveness, but specific intervention to improve phonological skills is important.

3. There appear to be different elements of phonological skill development which are successful. The emphasis on teaching onset and rime, and hence to aid children to read by recognising new words by analogy with ones they know, is promoted in the NLP, but the work of Deavers and Solity (1998) questions this. If their work is correct, the implication is to focus on letter–sound combinations before rime. This is in contradiction of the NLP approach, which might therefore be inappropriate. Further research here is necessary.

4. The nature of the tutor is important. Often, especially for children

with statements, a non-teaching assistant is provided. Such an aide might have many fine attributes, but they are rarely qualified teachers, yet important tasks regarding reading might be allocated to them. The evidence suggests that to optimise the construction and delivery of an effective programme, qualified teachers rather than teacher aides are important. Further, the teachers should be trained in delivery of such programmes.

5. Using tutors is not enough, the *content* of the programme also matters. Hence, there is an important interaction between content and delivery. The same will apply to whole-class teaching. It is not enough to proclaim that whole-class, didactic methods will work better; the lesson content and the detail of its delivery are also crucial elements.

6. Early intervention is indicated at the optimal period in the UK and US systems, namely around five to seven years in the UK. This raises important considerations, however. Firstly, it is arguable that it would be better to leave the intervention completely until later, and indeed that children should not be expected to learn to read until they are seven years plus. Reason (1998) argued that in Finland, where this is the norm, the children make better progress than in the UK. Unfortunately, even if this is a generalisable finding, it is currently untenable given the general expectation of Infant schools. Secondly, early intervention should be of high quality. The literacy hour may have many benefits, but the success of one-to-one tutoring is important for those children who are most at risk. Thirdly, early intervention might be sufficient for most, but not for all. A long-term support programme must therefore be set up for this minority. The literacy hour approach is likely to be too insensitive to this group's needs, especially after two to three years.

7. Fourthly, teacher attitudes and expectations are key elements. This is one of the foci for the National Literacy Strategy and we welcome this. While 'zero tolerance of under-performance' has an edge of new brutalism, the basic tenet is correct. However, in order to motivate children and teachers, and to ensure success, performance must be related to *appropriate* goals, *not* simply the goal that 80 per cent of children will gain the age expected score in the Key Stage 2 National Curriculum tests. The corollary is that 20 per cent will not – i.e. will fail. This is no more appropriate. Success for all can be achieved if it is defined appropriately and the interventions delivered effectively.

8. Finally, it is necessary to recognise the importance of assessment

and monitoring. The benefits of daily measurement are now well established, both as a source of motivation and as a means to ensure speedy amendments to a programme's content, goals or delivery. National Curriculum tests as a summative measure might have long-term evaluation uses, but they are useless in the daily educational process.

If baseline assessment is to be useful, the identification of children having, or at risk of having difficulties must be followed by effective intervention. The government's National Literacy Strategy has many positive points. However, in order to gain optimal benefits there should be greater attention paid to all the evidence on how children develop literacy, and on the relative effectiveness of approaches and intervention.

Chapter 9

Looking to the future

In Chapter 1 we identified eight possible purposes of school entry assessment at five years. These include purposes which were essentially child-oriented, including the early identification of learning difficulties and special educational needs. Alternatively baseline assessment could be used to provide information relevant to the school level, whether limited to accountability or used to aid school improvement programmes. We also demonstrated that the balance under the previous government was on the latter, school level purpose, even if much of the rhetoric had initially promoted baseline assessment as a means of helping individual children's development, as shown for example, in Sir Ron Dearing's Foreword to the draft proposals, where the only reference to purpose concerns the individual child:

> Finding out what children already know and are capable of as soon as they enter the reception class is an essential element in being able to give them the education they need to progress quickly in these important early years. (SCAA 1996b, p.1)

This purpose was later enshrined in the 1997 Education Act which stated:

> 'Baseline Assessment Scheme' means a scheme designed to enable pupils in a maintained primary school to be assessed for the purpose of assisting the future planning of their education and the measurement of their future educational achievements.

We have explored the government's actions as well as their rhetoric. In this concluding chapter we shall examine the implications for schools, given how the scheme has been developed. We shall offer suggestions to guide schools when making judgements and choosing a scheme, and also argue for future developments in this field.

The Government's position

Baseline assessment was developed as a central government initiative, through the agency of SCAA, towards the end of the Conservative administration. However, during that period, and subsequently, the Labour party were supportive of this development. This section of the 1997 Act received cross-party support and the new government has carried forward the requirements for baseline assessment to be conducted on all children entering schools from September 1998.

Interpreting the present government's intention is not simple. At one level they are very committed to the notion of improving standards, particularly of basic literacy and numeracy, and are seemingly at ease with the continuation of the centralisation of control that was developed under the Tories. The National Literacy Hour as well as baseline assessment are examples of central government's control of areas previously considered the province of schools.

On the other hand, the government did produce a Green Paper on special educational needs *Excellence for All Children* (DfEE 1997b), and launched a working group to explore how arts education may be promoted (DfEE Press Release 60/98, 4 February 1998). Hence, although the primary focus might be on improving basic standards, there is recognition that this is complex when taking account of the diversity of our children, and also that education should be broader, and valued as a more comprehensive experience, than a '3Rs curriculum'.

The main concern for baseline assessment is the relative emphasis to be placed on using information to support and promote the learning of individuals, or a class, as opposed to the education system as a whole. This is not a trivial distinction. The two processes are logically connected. For example, if the standards of individuals are raised, then the aggregated standard of our children as a whole will also improve. There are, however, more subtle difficulties as we have shown.

Promotion of improved educational outcomes

Within health there is now a new orientation of *health promotion*: the focus on promoting good health rather than identifying and keeping under surveillance children with ill health. This might be the prevention of a disease, or disorder, and be achieved for example by immunisation, prevention of accidents, or advice to parents. Within education, primary prevention has two elements. The first is outside its control, but improved medical services and pre-school provision might lead to a reduction in the numbers of children entering school with developmental problems (see Chapter 2).

From the education system perspective, primary prevention means the improvement of education for children to prevent failure or difficulties. This is the agenda of the White Paper *Excellence in Schools* (DfEE 1997a) and the intentions of the government that all schools should have targets which specify higher levels of attainment than are currently achieved. This is an admirable objective and matches the health service approach, e.g. Health 2000. If we can improve the educational opportunities for children in general, the theory goes, then we should reduce the numbers who are designated as having special educational needs. Support for this come in two forms. Firstly, there are the results of the National Curriculum assessments which suggest that standards have improved in many schools over three years. We have been critical of these in Chapter 5, but we must also consider their positive side. If it is indeed the case that standards are rising (the data currently are derived from post-Key Stage 1 assessments), then this is welcome news. It remains to be seen whether Key Stage 1 data will show the same increase, but in principle this could occur.

The results of initiatives such as that currently underway at the University of Warwick (Solity 1998) and the National Literacy Strategy (Literacy Task Force 1997), if successful, will reduce the numbers of children with low attainments in literacy, which might also reduce the number of children exhibiting behaviour problems as the two are often associated. Of course, it is possible that such initiatives might improve literacy but have the results that some critics fear, namely that the children will be demotivated and 'turned off', leading to more literate but more difficult pupils! Our own view is that this is the less likely option. Certainly reports of such initiatives often do not include data on changes in the children's behaviour but where these do appear these changes may be positive

The issue for our present discussion is: how might baseline assessment help with the promotion of improved educational outcomes? The first set of child-focused aims are based on the assumption that knowledge of *individuals*' current learning status is helpful in optimising future educational opportunities. This view has a long tradition in education, and underlies the child-centred approach. This has received much criticism over the past 20 years, but much has been ill-informed. The suggestion that this approach leads to children 'doing as they like' and schools having no plans or schemes/programmes of work is suspect. Certainly these

137

characteristics do not follow, and reports such as those by Her Majesty's Inspectors have shown that this view of what primary schools generally are like is not supported by the evidence.

Of more legitimate concern is the question of optimisation of children's learning by appropriate teaching, together with necessary resources. The danger is that this focus on teaching will be simplistic. It is easy to promote or require a 'literacy hour'. The guidelines, as we have shown, are largely sound but there are important omissions with respect to children's learning. Hence, a key role for baseline assessment is to identify the current status of children's learning, and help to guide future teaching over the short to medium term. For this to be successful, baseline assessment must address the range of children's educational development, and be part of a system of identification–assessment–teaching, as we presented in Chapter 3.

Furthermore, despite the understandable position of government trying to keep down costs, resources cannot be ignored. Indeed, the issue of class size has been identified by the present government as important, and presumably causative in children's learning. Finance has been allocated to enable class size for young children to be reduced, and this has the blessing of the Chief Inspector. Ironically, this is an area which might not be supported by the evidence. The simple approach is to view class size and quality of teaching as the key, but separate issues. What also should be examined is the interaction between size of the teaching group, optimal approach to teaching, and outcomes. For example, rather than reduce class size across the board – remember, some schools in pre-LMS days had small classes owing to positive action – it might be better to target resources *and* teaching methods. Our review of one-to-one tutoring has indicated the success of this. There is also the use of small groups of two to four children. The National Literacy strategy might allow a variety of educational opportunities to occur, but these will need to be related to a clear plan of action.

This approach is systemic, recognising the needs of individuals, but addressing a significant element of intervention at the system. Identifying individuals' current learning needs does not require that a proportion of children be designated as having 'special' educational needs. Rather, an approach which promotes optimal standards, and rate of progress might allow for different starting points and differential rates and trajectories of progress.

If this approach is taken, the use of baseline assessment remains fundamentally for the good of individuals, and will be designed with this in mind. As we argued in Chapters 3 and 4, there are major problems in trying to design a system that allows useful measurement both for the purpose of teaching, and accountability. However, the focus on school improvement does fit into a systemic approach. The technical limitations of the measures might be taken into account *within* schools in order to guide policy development. The trouble comes when shaky statistics are used as measures for accountability via the use of value-added analyses.

Implications for schools and LEAs

Every school from September 1998 must have a baseline assessment scheme for all its school entrants around five years. According to the QCA (February 1998) there are likely to be over 80 schemes accredited for this first cohort. How should a school choose an appropriate scheme? We offer the following guidance when choosing a scheme, but first we must re-emphasise the importance of distinguishing purpose. To some extent decisions on this will be outside the realm of influence of the school, being determined by central government. For example, it will be a requirement that the scheme produces 'one or more numerical outcomes capable of being used later for value added analysis' (SCAA 1997d, p.6). Nevertheless, as we have tried to show, there are a number of questions about the quality of a scheme which should be addressed. The following suggestions are offered to aid schools in choosing an appropriate baseline assessment scheme.

1. **LEA approval.** The LEA might have undertaken a review of schemes, and might even have developed its own. The LEA may prefer schools to use this, to enable comparison of results. This is reasonable, but must be subject to an evaluation of any recommended scheme.
2. **SCAA/QCA accreditation.** SCAA, now the QCA, must accredit any scheme which will be in use. By February 1998, 47 schemes had been accredited in the first round, and another 45 had been submitted or re-submitted. The expectation was that over 80 schemes would be accredited for use. Given the nature of the criteria, and the assistance of SCAA/QCA in advising potential scheme providers of actions to take to meet the criteria, it was expected that most will be able to meet those specifications. (The accreditation criteria are set out in Chapter 1, Figure 1.2.)
3. **Technical quality.** The QCA criteria do not specify technical quality. We consider this to be unacceptable and recommend that any schemes shall meet at least minimum standards.

- The scheme should provide evidence that it has been standardised and that its reliability and validity have been evaluated.
- Further, there should be evidence on the characteristics of the scheme, including the standardisation sample (size, gender and ethnic/first language distributions), its reliability, both over a short period of time and comparing the same child's scores when assessed by two assessors.
- Finally, the evidence provided should include an acceptable standard of quality. For example
  - the standardisation sample should be representative of at least one LEA, if not a national sample, and comprise at least 500 to 1,000 pupils
  - reliabilities of total scores should be at least 0.8 to 0.9
  - the measure should have a coherent structure.
- Evidence on predictive validity is less likely and is inherently more problematic. It should not be a requirement now. However, evidence on this dimension should be a requirement after two to three years (i.e. from 2001) and schemes which provide satisfactory evidence of this are to be welcomed.

4. **Monitoring and evaluation.** To be acceptable, a scheme should be subject to ongoing evaluation, which will allow feedback to schools.

Child-focused issues

In addition to these general points, a baseline assessment scheme may provide satisfactory evidence that it can serve as a support for the school's attempts to meet the primary aim of the Education Act 1997, which specifies that a scheme 'must be designed to enable pupils at a maintained primary school to be assessed for the purpose of assisting the future planning of their education'. It is necessary to consider the following.

5. **Identification of children with SEN.** The scheme should accurately identify children who require additional assessment and extra attention. We have been critical of the concept of 'special educational needs', but this term is used here owing to its general currency. The main issue is that the scheme should identify children having difficulties, whatever the cause, and link with the school's SEN register and scheme for identification and assessment of children under the Code of Practice.

6. **Identification of children's difficulties.** The scheme may go further than simply categorise a child as 'OK'/'not OK'. A better scheme will provide the beginning of a set of information allowing a picture of the child's pattern of difficulties, and their strengths, to be built up. Baseline assessment schemes should provide such a profile, but with evidence of their validity.

7. **Monitoring all children's learning.** Baseline assessment should be an aid to the monitoring of all children, providing the first stage within the Infant school. The scheme should allow teachers to make initial judgements, building upon information from pre-school and home, of all their class with respect to their educational needs.

8. **Links with intervention.** The scheme must be directly linked to planning for intervention. In practice, a baseline assessment scheme is essentially a screening procedure, hence it must be followed by a more thorough series of assessments in order to determine appropriate intervention. Nevertheless, the baseline assessment should provide initial indications for this assessment – intervention process, for example by indicating whether a child has difficulties across all areas of development, is developing across the board at an advanced rate, or has a more complex profile, in which case indications of specific difficulties should be provided.

School-focus

We identified four potential purposes at the school level. Two are public (accountability and budget determination), while the other two allow information to be restricted to within-school initiatives (resource planning and school improvement). Schools, and LEAs, will have no choice but to have a scheme which will allow an accountability measure using value-added analysis, so we shall focus on this purpose.

The criteria 1–4 specified above are all relevant, but there are different aspects.

9. **Resource planning.** The scheme should allow the beginning of a differentiated planning of resources depending upon the needs of identified children. Overall resources will be fixed, or substantially so, and some initiatives might also be imposed (e.g. the literacy hour). There is still potential for variation of interventions in accord with the approaches to intervention outlined in Chapter 8, for example:

- use of whole-class, groups and one-to-one tutoring
- peer tutoring (using older pupils for five year olds)
- parent involvement – for whom, and for what purpose.

10. **Budget allocation.** If LEA budget formulae are to be influenced by baseline assessment, high accuracy and validity are required. We recommend the scheme be run in parallel to the existing scheme (e.g. free school meals entitlement) for at least two to three years, gradually modifying the budget allocation.

11. **Accountability.** For a value-added analysis to be undertaken, schools need to be assured that the baseline assessment is providing a true picture of its intake, *and* that National Curriculum tests provide a valid picture of learners from Key Stage 1. If one or both of these is untrue, schools cannot be assured that the relative 'gains' or 'losses' of their children are real. The evidence so far suggests that very large variations may be found between schools in their pupils' progress but the school factors are not yet clear. Schools would be advised to use a scheme which allows a range of additional information to be collected, and to run the scheme over several years as an experiment. The present level of evidence does not allow schools to make definitive judgements on causality of relative pupil progress and value-added.

12. **School improvement.** As with resource planning, accuracy is important but less critical. Measures should be valid and reliable, but some variations can lead to further debate, analysis and more investigation in the spirit of enquiry, *not* to 'cover your back'. For example, a baseline assessment scheme which inflates children's skills at five years will lead to an under estimate of development by seven years – a potential nightmare if results are published as 'value-added', as the school's contribution to its pupils' development will be underestimated. If this information is used within-school only, then it becomes an indication of the need to moderate scores, and choose another baseline assessment scheme. The former will lead to cover up, the latter to reflection, openness and collaboration.

Parents

Baseline assessment schemes are required to provide guidance explaining the outcomes to parents. However, our analysis indicates that this is more complex than this instruction implies. Also, our preference is that parents be partners, not simply recipients of information (see also Wolfendale 1998).

Parents are able to provide important information prior to school entry and as the child settles. This will help inform teachers' initial practice, and baseline assessment should add to that. Discussion of findings should be interactive, a chance for teacher and parents to consider the implications of the baseline assessment outcomes and of the information provided by the parents and teacher – and indeed by the child. This model, of sharing evidence and thoughts, developing understanding, and then planning future action, requires valid measures and information which is more than a numerical outcome.

This obligation to interact with parents and to depend on valid data applies also to value-added analyses. Here the information may concern a child whose progress is assessed. Or it may concern the school – its relative value-added. In either case we have a responsibility to provide accurate and fair information.

The future

Baseline assessment is here to stay, at least for the next five to ten years. Looking back over the past two decades it is interesting to note the development from systems of early identification of children with learning difficulties to a system primarily designed, it appears, to hold schools accountable for the relative value they add to their pupils' learning.

What is common, and depressingly so, is the continuing lack of interest in, or recognition of, the technical quality of the instruments used. The early work of one of us (Lindsay) included criticisms of this tendency in the 1970s and 1980s, often characterised by LEAs setting up teams of teachers, with support from advisors, to produce a method which had a face validity – but then not undertaking basic evaluation of the scheme that arose. There were exceptions such as the Infant Rating Scale in Sheffield (Lindsay 1981) and the Early Infant Check in Bury (Pearson and Quinn 1986), but many others were developed but not evaluated.

As social scientists we condemn this approach, which would simply not be tolerated in other domains. For example, health is becoming increasingly rigorous. In addition to research into drug effectiveness and safety, there is a substantial move towards evidence-based treatments where the effectiveness of different approaches are evaluated. The comparison with education gives concern. The National Literacy Strategy was presented, with statements of expectations for teaching, and assertions about good practice – yet no evidence was provided, and areas of research were neglected.

In our own work (e.g. *Infant Index*, Desforges and Lindsay 1995a, *Baseline-Plus*, Desforges and Lindsay with Edexcel 1998) we have

143

attempted to do two things. Firstly, we have sought to produce schemes which match the purpose identified by teachers. Secondly, we have developed schemes, with teachers, and then evaluated their quality. We have also maintained a programme of research to continue the evaluation process. We have also highlighted the limitations as well as the strengths of our own schemes, as well as those of others.

Optimising children's learning is a fundamental objective of the education system. In the early years (three to eight years) we bridge between the home and school, and learning by informal means and increased levels of instruction and direction. Baseline assessment has, potentially, a very important part to play in this process but, and it is a major proviso, the process must be appropriate and have the confidence of all those who will use, or be subject to it.

We must not set up systems which label children inappropriately as having special educational needs, or which miss those who do have difficulties, resulting in their needs not being met. Neither must we have a system which falsely attributes success to some schools, and failure to others on the basis of faulty measurement tools. The introduction of baseline assessment provides an opportunity to add to our understanding of children's development, school effectiveness, and the factors which contribute to each – but only if the approach is recognised as exploratory and experimental. While politicians may like certainties and data expressed in absolute terms, the position with baseline assessment does not allow this. Furthermore, the decision to allow more than one scheme, unlike the common measure of key stage assessments, renders comparisons between schools using diferent schemes problematic. If there will indeed be over 80 baseline assessment schemes, then comparisons of schools other than with those using the same scheme will be a nonsense.

We have tried to set out the dangers as well as approaches to solutions. A degree of humility is required. In contrast to a focus on certainties, we stress the variability of children's development and the need to match these different potential trajectories with appropriate teaching. Our aims are to enhance standards, but for all children; to promote optimal learning rather than attribute deficit explanations of failure.

In its 1997 Green Paper the government gave a lead to similar objectives, but the requirements for baseline assessment do not ensure that the technical issues be addressed. Faith in an approach is welcome, but not sufficient in the absence of good quality evidence. Baseline assessment does have an important place, but the measures to be used must be sound if we are to contribute to the government's intention to promote 'Excellence for All Children'.

References

Audit Commission (1995) *Local Authority Performance Indicators 1994/95. Volumes 1 and 2*. London: HMSO.

Audit Commission and Her Majesty's Inspection (1992) *Getting in on the Act*. London: HMSO.

Birmingham City Council (1996a) *Baseline Assessment*. Birmingham: Local Education Authority.

Birmingham City Council (1996b) *Baseline Assessment for the Primary Phase – Autumn 1995*. Report of the Chief Education Officer to Education (Service Review and Monitoring) Sub-Committee, 25 June 1996. Birmingham: Local Education Authority.

Black, P. (1996) 'Formative assessment and the improvement of learning', *British Journal of Special Education* **23**, 51–6.

Blatchford, P. and Cline, T. (1992) 'Baseline assessment for school entrants', *Research Papers in Education* **7**, 247–69.

Blatchford, P. *et al.* (1987) 'Associations between pre-school reading related skills and later reading achievement', *British Educational Research Journal* **13**(1), 15–23.

Bowlby, J. (1969) *Attachment and Loss. Volume 1 Attachment*. Harmondsworth: Penguin.

Broadfoot, P. *et al.* (1989) *Records of Achievement. Report of the National Evaluation*. London: HMSO.

Bronfenbrenner, U. (1979) *The Ecology of Human Behaviour*. Cambridge, Mass.: Harvard University Press.

Caspall, L., Sainsbury, M., Cropper, A. (1997) *Trials of Baseline Assessment Scales: Report 3*. Slough: NFER.

Cato, V. and Whetton, C. (1991) *An Enquiry into LEA Evidence on Standards of Reading of Seven Year Old Children*. Windsor: NFER.

Clarke, A. D. and Clarke, A. M. (1985) 'Constancy and change in the growth of human characteristics', *Annual Progress in Child Psychiatry and Child Development 1985*, 27–52.

Clay, M. M. (1985) *The Early Detection of Reading Difficulties (3rd edition)*. Auckland: Heinemann.

Cochrane, A. and Holland, W. (1969) 'Validation of screening procedures', *British Medical Journal* **27**, 3–8.

Coltheart, M. and Jackson, N. E. (1998) 'Defining dyslexia', *Child Psychology and Psychiatry Review* **3**, 12–16.

Cox, C. B. and Dyson, A. E. (1971) *The Black Papers on Education*. London: David-Poynter.

Croll, P. and Moses, D. (1985) *One in Five: The Assessment and Incidence of Special Educational Needs*. London: Routledge and Kegan Paul.

Daly, T. (1997) 'Targets, targets, targets.' Unpublished M.Sc. dissertation, University of Sheffield.

Daniel, F. (1996) 'SATs, STATs and STA.' Unpublished M.Sc. dissertation, University of Sheffield.

Dearing, R. (1994) *The National Curriculum and its Assessment*. London: SCAA.

Deavers, R. and Solity, J. (1998) 'The role of rime units in early reading.' Paper presented to the Annual Conference of the Division of Educational and Child Psychology of the British Psychological Society, Bournemouth, January.

De Hirsch, K., Jansky, J. J., Langford, W. S. (1966) *Predicting Reading Failure*. New York: Harper and Row.

Department for Education (DfE) (1994) *The Code of Practice on the Identification and Assessment of Pupils with Special Educational Needs*. London: HMSO.

Department for Education and Employment (DfEE) (1997a) *Excellence in Schools*. London: DfEE.

Department for Education and Employment (1997b) *Excellence for All children*. London: DfEE.

Department for Education and Employment (1997c) *Teaching: High Status, High Standards: Requirements for Courses of Initial Teacher Training, Circular 10/97*. London: DfEE.

Department of Education and Science (DES) (1975) *A Language for Life* (The Bullock Report). London: HMSO.

Department of Education and Science (1978) *Special Education Needs* (The Warnock Report). London: HMSO.

Department of Education and Science (1987) *National Curriculum Task Group on Assessment and Testing*. London: HMSO.

Department of Education and Science (1991) *The Teaching and Learning of Reading in Primary Schools in 1991: A Report by HMI*. London: HMSO.

Derrington, C., Evans, C., Lee, B. (1996) *The Code in Practice: The Impact on Schools and LEAs*. Slough: NFER.

Desforges, M. (1991) 'National Curriculum assessment and primary records of achievement and experience: tensions and resolution', in Lindsay, G. and Miller, A. (eds) *Psychological Services for Primary Schools*. London: Longmans.

Desforges, M. (1995) 'Separation, divorce and the school', in Best, R., Lang, P., Lodge, C. and Watkins, C. (eds) *Pastoral Care and Personal and Social Education*. London: Cassell.

Desforges, M. and Lindsay, G. (1995a) *Infant Index*. London: Hodder and Stoughton.

Desforges, M. and Lindsay, G. (1995b) 'Baseline assessment', *Educational and Child Psychology* **12**, 42–51.

Desforges, M. and Lindsay, G. (1996) *Baseline Assessment at School Entry*. Sheffield: Sheffield LEA.

Desforges, M. and Lindsay, G. with Hodder & Stoughton (1998) *Baseline-Plus*. London: Edexcel.

Dockrell, J. and Lindsay, G. (1998) 'The ways in which speed and language difficulties impact on children's access to the curriculum', *Child Language Teaching and Therapy* **14**, 1–17.

Dockrell, J. and Messer, D. (1999) *Language and Communication Problems in Children*. London: Cassell.

Donaldson, M. (1978) *Children's Minds*. London: Fontana.

Douglas, J. W. B. (1964) *The Home and School*. London: Macgibbon and Kee.

Drummond, M. (1993) *Assessing Children's Learning*. London: David Fulton Publishers.

Erikson, E. (1968) *Identity, Youth and Crisis*. New York: Norton.

Essen, J. and Wedge, P. (1982) *Continuities in Childhood Disadvantage*. London: Heinemann.

Esser, G., Schmidt, M., Woener, W. (1990) 'Epidemiology and the course of psychiatric disorders in school age children', *Journal of Child Psychology and Psychiatry* **31**, 243–63.

Fitz-Gibbon, C. T. (1995) *Issues to be Considered in the Design of a National Value Added System*. Durham: Durham University, CEM Centre.

Fitz-Gibbon, C. T. (1997) *The Value Added National Project: Final Report*. London: School Curriculum and Assessment Authority.

Francis, B., Green, M., Payne, C. (1994) *The GLIM System of Generalised Linear Interactive Modelling*. Oxford: Clarendon Press.

Gessell, A. (1946) 'The Ontogenesis of Infant Behaviour', in Carmichael, L. (ed.) *Manual of Child Psychology*. New York: J. Wiley.

Glynn, T. (1987) 'More power to the parents: behavioural approaches to remedial tutoring at home', in Wheldall, K. (ed.) *The Behaviourist in the Classroom*. London: Allen & Unwin.

Graham, D. and Tytler, D. (1993) *A Lesson for us All*. London: Routledge.

Haggard, M. (1993) *Research in the Development of Effective Services for Hearing Impaired Children*. London: Nuffield Provincial Hospitals Trust.

Hall, D. M. B. (ed.) (1996) *Health for All Children*. Oxford: Oxford University Press.

Hatcher, P. J., Hulme, C., Ellis, A. W. (1994) 'Ameliorating early reading failure by integrating the teaching of reading and phonological skills: the Phonological Linkage Hypothesis', *Child Development* **65**, 41–57.

Her Majesty's Inspectors (1990) *The Teaching and Learning of Reading in Primary Schools*. London: HMSO.

Hindley, C. and Owen, C. F. (1978) 'The extent of individual changes in IQ for ages between 6 months and 17 years in a British longitudinal sample', *Journal of Child Psychology and Psychiatry*, 19, 329–50.

House of Commons Select Committee on Education (1987) Third Report from the Education, Science and Arts Committee: Special Educational Needs: Implementation of the Education Act 1981. London: HMSO.

Iverson, S. and Tunmer, W. E. (1993) 'Phonological processing skills and the Reading Recovery programme', *Journal of Educational Psychology* **85**, 112–26.

Jesson, D. (1996) *Value Added Measures of School GCSE Performance*. London: HMSO.

Lawton, D. (1988) 'Ideologies of education', in Lawton, D. and Chitty, C. (eds) *The National Curriculum*, Bedford Way Papers Number 3. London: University of London Institute of Education.

Lazo, M. G. and Pumfrey, P. D. (1996) 'Early predictors of later attainment in reading and spelling', *Reading* **30**(3), 5–11.

Lindsay, G. (1979) 'The early identification of learning difficulties and the monitoring of children's progress', unpublished PhD thesis, University of Birmingham.

Lindsay, G. (1980) 'The Infant Rating Scale', *British Journal of Educational Psychology* **50**, 97–104.

Lindsay, G. (1981) *The Infant Rating Scale*. Sevenoaks: Hodder and Stoughton.

147

Lindsay, G. (ed.) (1984) *Screening for Children with Special Needs*. Beckenham: Croom Helm.

Lindsay, G. (1996) 'Quality and educational psychology services', in Watson, K., Modgil, C., Modgil, S. (eds) *Educational Dilemmas: Debate and Diversity. Volume 4: Quality in Education*. London: Cassell.

Lindsay, G. (1997a) 'Values and legislation', in Lindsay, G. and Thompson, D. (eds) *Values into Practice in Special Education*. London: David Fulton Publishers.

Lindsay, G. (1997b) 'Open dialogue: peer review': reply to Raven, *Education Section Review* 21, 19–23.

Lindsay, G. (1998) 'Baseline assessment: a positive or malign initiative?', in Norwich, B. and Lindsay, G. (eds) *Baseline Assessment*. Tamworth: NASEN.

Lindsay, G. and Wedell, K. (1982) 'The early identification of educationally "at risk" children' (revised), *Journal of Learning Difficulties* 15, 212–17.

Lindsay, G., Evans, A., Jones, B. (1984) 'Paired reading versus relaxed reading: a comparison', *British Journal of Educational Psychology* 55, 303–09.

Literacy Task Force (1997) *The Implementation of the National Literacy Strategy*. London: DfEE.

Locke, J. (1997) 'A theory of neurolinguistic development', *Brain and Language* 58, 265–326.

Marsh, A. (1997) *Current Practice for Resourcing Additional Educational Needs in Local Educational Authorities*. Slough: NFER.

Moffitt, T. *et al.* (1993) 'The natural history of change in intellectual performance', *Journal of Child Psychology and Psychiatry* 34, 455–506.

Morissey, P. (1997) 'Baseline assessment: a study of the predictive validity of the Infant Index', unpublished M.Sc. thesis, University of Sheffield.

Mortimore, P. *et al.* (1988) *School Matters: The Junior Years*. London: Open Books.

Nicholson, R. I. (1996) 'Developmental dyslexia: past, present and future', *Dyslexia* 2, 190–207.

Nicholson R. and Fawcett, A. (1996) *The Dyslexia Early Screening Test*. Kent: Psychological Corporation.

Norwich, B. (1996) 'Special needs education or education for all: connective specialisation and ideologised impurity', *British Journal of Special Education* 23, 100–103.

Nutbrown, C. (1997) *Recognising Early Literacy Development*. London: Paul Chapman Publishing.

Office for Standards in Education (OFSTED) (1998a) *Changes to the National Curriculum in Key Stages 1 and 2: Implications for Primary and Secondary School Inspections*. London: OFSTED.

Office for Standards in Education (1998b) *The Annual Report of Her Majesty's Chief Inspector of Schools 1996–97*. London: HMSO.

Office for Standards in Education and the Teacher Training Agency (1997) *Framework for the Assessment of Quality and Standards in Initial Teacher Training 1997/98*. London: OFSTED/TTA.

Office of Her Majesty's Chief Inspector of Schools (OHMCI) (1997) *The SEN Code of Practice Two Years On: HMI 23*. London: OFSTED.

Pearson, L. and Quinn, J. (1986) *The Bury Checklist*. Windsor: NFER-Nelson.

Peters, T. J. and Waterhouse, R. H. (1982) *In Search of Excellence*. New York: Harper & Row.

Piaget, J. (1953) *The Origins of Intelligence in Children*. London: Routledge and Kegan Paul.

Pocock, S. J., Smith, M., Baghurst, P. (1994) 'Environmental lead and children's intelligence: a systematic review of the epidemiological evidence', *British Medical Journal* **309**, 1189–97.

Pumfrey, P. D. and Elliott, C. D. (1992) 'Objective testing: insights or illusions?', in Pumfrey, P. (ed.) *Reading Standards: Issues and Evidence*. Leicester: British Psychological Society, Division of Educational and Child Psychology.

Pumfrey, P. D. and Reason, R. (1991) *Specific Learning Difficulties (Dyslexia): Challenges and Responses*. London: Routledge.

Raven, J. (1997) 'Open dialogue: education, educational research, ethics and the BPS', *Education Section Review* **21**, 3–11.

Reason, R. (1998) 'Phonics for all: an overkill or a balanced approach to literacy?' Paper presented to the Annual Course of the Division of Educational and Child Psychology of the British Psychological Society, Bournemouth, January.

Richards, C. (1997) *Primary Education, Standards and Ofsted. Towards a more authentic conversation*. Centre for Research in Primary Education, University of Warwick.

Riddick, B. (1996) *Living with Dyslexia*. London: Routledge.

Rigby, A. *et al.* (1997) 'Matching health and education data: does a mother's postnatal depression predict impaired performance in her children at entry to infant school.' *Proceedings of the Royal College of Paediatrics and Child Health Annual Meeting. Volume 1*, 82.

Ross, S. M. *et al.* (1995) 'Increasing the academic success of disadvantaged children: an examination of alternative early intervention programmes', *American Educational Research Journal* **32**, 773–800.

Rutter, M. (1981) *Maternal Deprivation Reassessed*. Harmondsworth: Penguin.

Rutter, M. and Rutter, M. (1992) *Developing Minds*. London: Penguin.

Rutter, M., Tizard, J., Whitmore, K. (1970) *Education, Health and Behaviour*. London: Longman.

Rutter, M. *et al.* (1979) *Fifteen Thousand Hours*. London: Open Books.

Sampson, O. (1980) *Child Guidance: Its History, Provenance and Future*. Leicester: British Psychological Society.

Schools Curriculum and Assessment Authority (SCAA) (1996a) *Nursery Education. Desirable Outcomes for Children's Learning*. London: DfEE.

Schools Curriculum and Assessment Authority (1996b) *Baseline Assessment: Draft Proposals*. London: SCAA.

Schools Curriculum and Assessment Authority (1996c) *Trials of Baseline Assessment Schemes: Report 1*. London: SCAA.

Schools Curriculum and Assessment Authority (1996d) *Trials of Baseline Assessment Schemes: Report 2*. London: SCAA.

Schools Curriculum and Assessment Authority (1997a) *Target Setting and Benchmarking in Schools – A Consultation Paper*. London: SCAA.

Schools Curriculum and Assessment Authority (1997b) *Baseline Assessment Scales*. Cm/97/809. London: SCAA.

Schools Curriculum and Assessment Authority (1997c) *SCAA Consultation on Baseline Assessment: Report January 1997*. London: SCAA.

Schools Curriculum and Assessment Authority (1997d) *The National Framework for Baseline Assessment: Criteria and Procedures for the Accreditation of Baseline*

Assessment Schemes. London: SCAA.

Schools Curriculum and Assessment Authority (1997e) *Looking at Children's Learning*. Cm/97/865. London: SCAA.

Sheffield LEA (1993) *Sheffield Records of Primary Education and Achievement*. Sheffield: LEA.

Sheffiel LEA (1997) *Local Management of Schools: Budget Statement 1997–98*. Sheffield: LEA.

Siegel, L. S. (1992) 'An evaluation of the discrepancy definition of dyslexia', *Journal of Learning Disabilities* **25**, 617–88.

Solity, J. (1998) 'The Early Reading research: raising literacy attainments in the early years.' Paper presented to the Annual Course of the Division of Educational and Child Psychology of the British Psychological Society, Bournemouth, January.

Spencer, N. (1996) *Poverty and Child Health*. Oxford: Radcliffe Medical Press.

Stanovich, K. E. (1994) 'Does dyslexia exist?', *Journal of Child Psychology and Psychiatry* **35**, 579–96.

Stanovich, K. E. (1998) 'Refining the phonological core deficit model', *Child Psychology and Psychiatry Review* **3**, 17–21.

Stanovich, K. E. and Stanovich, P. J. (1997) 'Further thoughts on aptitude/ achievement discrepancy', *Educational Psychology in Practice* **13**, 3–8.

Strand, S. (1996) 'Value added analysis of the 1995 Key Stage 1 results: an LEA case study', in Platts, G. (ed.) *LEA's Value Added and School Improvement*. Manchester: Society of Education Offices.

Strand, S. (1997) 'Pupil progress during Key Stage 1: a value added analysis of school effects', *British Educational Research Journal* **23**, 471–87.

Streetly, A. *et al.* (1994) 'Variation in coverage by ethnic group of neonatal (Guthrie) screening programme in South London', *British Medical Journal* **309**, 373–4.

Stuart, M. (1995) 'Prediction and qualitative assessment of the five- and six-year-old children's reading: a longitudinal study', *British Journal of Educational Psychology* **65**, 287–96.

Sylva, K. and Hurry, J. (1995) *Early Intervention in Children with Reading Difficulties*. London: SCAA.

Topping, K. (1988) *The Peer Tutoring Handbook*. London: Croom Helm.

Topping, K. and Lindsay, G. (1992) 'Paired reading: A review of the literature', *Research Papers in Education* **7**, 199–246.

Trower, P. and Vincent, L. (1995) *The Value Added National Project. Technical Report: Secondary*. Durham: University of Durham, CEM Centre.

Tymms, P. (1996) *Baseline Assessment and Value Added: Report to SCAA*. London: SCAA.

Tymms, P. (1997a) 'PIPs Baseline and Value Added', unpublished paper, Durham University, CEM Centre.

Tymms, P. (1997b) *The Value Added National Project: Technical Report: Primary 3*. London: SCAA.

Tymms, P. (1997c) *The Value Added National Project. Technical Report: Primary 4*. Durham: University of Durham, CEM Centre.

Tymms, P. and Henderson, B. (1995) *The Value Added National Project. Technical Report: Primary*. Durham: Durham University, CEM Centre.

Tymms, P. and Merrell, C. (1997) *Reception Assessment 1996–97*. Durham: University of Durham, CEM Centre.

Tymms, P., Merrell, C., Henderson, B. (1995) *The Reception Year: A Quantitative Investigation of the Attainment and Progress of Pupils*. Durham: University of Durham, CEM Centre.

Tymms, P., Merrell, C., Henderson, B. (1997) 'The first year at school: a quantitative investigation of the attainment and progress of pupils', *Education Research and Evaluation* **3**, 101–18.

Vellutino, F. R. *et al.* (1996) 'Cognitive profiles of difficult-to-remediate and readily remediated poor readers: early intervention as a vehicle for distinguishing between cognitive and experiential deficits as basic causes of specific reading disability', *Journal of Educational Psychology* **88**, 601–38.

Vincent, D. and de la Mare, M. (1990) *Individual Reading Analysis*. Windsor: NFER-Nelson.

Wandsworth LEA (1992) *Baseline Assessment Handbook*. London Borough of Wandsworth, Education Department.

Wasik, B. A. and Slavin, R. E. (1993) 'Preventing early reading failure within one-to-one tutoring: a review of five programs', *Reading Research Quarterly* **28**, 179–200.

Wedell, K. (1978) 'Early identification and compensatory interaction.' Paper presented at the NATO International Conference on Learning Disorders, Ottawa.

Wedell, K. and Lindsay, G. (1980) 'Early identification procedures: what have we learned?', *Remedial Education* **15**, 130–35.

Wedell, K. and Raybould, E. C. (1976) 'The early identification of educationally "at risk" children', *Educational Review, Occasional Publication No 6*. Birmingham: University of Birmingham.

Wells, G. and Raban, B. (1978) *Children Learning to Read*. Final report to the Social Science Research Council.

Wilkinson, J. E. and Napuk, A. (1997) *Baseline Assessment: A Review of Literature*. Glasgow: University of Glasgow, Department of Education.

Wilson, J. M. G. and Junger, G. (1968) *Principles and Practice of Screening for Disease*. Public Health Papers No 34. Geneva: World Health Organisation.

Wolfendale, S. (1990) *All About Me*. Nottingham: NES-Arnold.

Wolfendale, S. (1993) *Baseline Assessment: A review of current practice, issues and strategies for effective implementation*. Stoke on Trent: Trentham Books.

Wolfendale, S. (1998) 'Baseline assessment in respect of special educational needs, parental involvement and equal opportunities', in Norwich, B. and Lindsay, G. (eds) *Baseline Assessment*. Tamworth: NASEN.

Wolfendale, S. and Bryans, T. (1979) *Identification of Learning Difficulties: A Model for Implementation*. London: National Association for Remedial Education.

151

Index